SEDIMENTOLOGY BOOK **1**

Processes *and* Analysis

D1439411

Chris King

LONGMAN

The Author

CHRIS KING is Head of Geology at Altrincham Grammar School for Boys, where he also co-ordinates the teaching of Science in the lower school. He teaches A-level Geology to boys from this school and to girls from the nearby Altrincham Grammar School for Girls. He is currently Chairman of the Earth Science Teachers' Association, and has been Chairman of the Association's Curriculum Working Group. He is also a member of the Joint Matriculation Board A-level Geology committees. His practical experience of Sedimentology includes five years spent prospecting for diamonds in Africa and Australia.

ISBN 0 582 02200 2

First published 1992

Fourth impression 1994
© Longman Group UK Ltd

Set in 11 on 12pt Times

Produced through Longman Malaysia, PA

Contents

Acknowledgements

I would like to thank Peter Kennett and John McManus for their sterling work in commenting upon, and improving, the manuscript. Peter Kennett's encouragement throughout has been particularly valuable. James Hooke, Lloyd Boardman and Martin Smith made very helpful comments upon certain sections of the work and I would like to thank them as well. Any errors remaining in the book are entirely my own.

I would also like to thank Helen Busteed for her careful drafting of the diagrams, and Keith Nodding, Headmaster of Altrincham Grammar School for Boys, for providing me with working facilities.

Finally, without the support of my wife and young family, these books would not have been written and I thank them for their continuing encouragement.

Chris King

Preface

This book has been designed, together with its companion book *Sedimentology Book 2, The Depositional Environments*, to provide all the material necessary for the study of Sedimentology at sixth-form level, and to provide useful background material for college and university students beginning courses in Geology or Earth Science.

The two books cover all the core topics relating to surface processes and sedimentary rocks that are contained in existing A- and AS-level Geology syllabuses. This material will also be of value in the teaching of those aspects of Sedimentology and related topics that are expected to appear in the sixth-form Earth Science courses of the near future. In addition, those studying Physical Geography will find many sections of the books helpful.

Also covered are many of the economic aspects of Sedimentology, including the supplies of raw materials and fossil fuels that are so vital to the economy of the British Isles. The sedimentary environments discussed are related to examples of such environments from the geological past, thus illustrating how evidence for the movement of the region over geological time is preserved in rocks. In this way, many of the elements of Stratigraphy and Economic Geology present in Geology courses are covered.

The organisation of the material is such that different economic aspects are linked, chapter by chapter, into the appropriate parts of the text. For those wishing to concentrate on specific topics in Economic Geology, it is recommended that the relevant sub-sections be studied in the order given below.

Coal	Coal Swamps and Coal Measures	Book 2, p. 69
	Swamp Deposits to Coal	Book 1, p. 79
Coastal erosion	Coastal Defences	Book 2, p. 68
	Cliff Retreat	Book 1, p. 35
Heavy mineral deposits		
	Heavy Mineral Accumulations	Book 1, p. 35
	Diamond Prospecting	
	in Ancient Braided Streams	Book 2, p. 31
	Placer Gold in South Africa	Book 2, p. 32
Oil and gas	Oil Source Rocks	Book 2, p. 103
	The Formation of Oil and Gas	Book 1, p. 80
	Oil and Gas Reservoir Rocks	Book 1, p. 61
	Oil and Gas Reservoir Shapes	Book 1, p. 72
	Hydrocarbons in Deltas	Book 2, p. 71
	Hydrocarbons in Submarine Fans and	
	Turbidite Deposits	Book 2, p. 103
	Evaporite and Hydrocarbon Reservoirs	Book 2, p. 73

Practical work is an important element in science courses, and AS-level Geology syllabuses contain a significant practical element. Practical approaches should be an important part of A-level courses in Geology too, and in future syllabus changes the requirement for practical work is likely to be increased. Investigational practical work will probably also become a more significant part of degree courses in the future. Fieldwork is another essential element of all Geology and Earth Science courses, and the investigational aspects of fieldwork are also likely to be highlighted in future curriculum developments. It is with these factors in mind that the sections on *Practical Investigation and Fieldwork* have been devised. It is hoped that they will be of great value to student and teacher alike.

The sections entitled *Test Your Understanding* have been included, together with the questions in the figure captions, to encourage students to consider and evaluate the understanding they have gained from the text, and to apply it in new and different circumstances. This is precisely the approach used by professional and academic geologists during their exploration and research.

Geology and Earth Science have proved to be very rewarding areas of study for young people and adults alike, with many going on to careers in these fields or gaining hobbies for life. In both cases the approach used is that of the 'rock detective' as described in Chapter 1. Now that Earth Science has become an important element in school science syllabuses for 5- to 16-year-olds, we may expect that many more students will choose to study Earth Science in the future. One thing is certain: studies in Earth Science, including their sedimentological aspects, will continue to be vital to the economy of the British Isles, to the economy of the world, and to the conservation of the environment and resources of our planet, well into the twenty-first century and beyond.

Please note: all instances of the pronoun 'he' are to be interpreted as referring equally to both men and women.

1. THE WORK OF THE DETECTIVE ON ANCIENT ROCKS

The Background

For thousands of years man accepted rocks as rocks, plain and simple. Rocks were just there. You saw them in cliffs and on mountain tops and found them if you dug down into the ground. They could be useful, forming caves to live in or, later, as good foundations and building stones. They could provide valuable materials such as iron, tin and coal. They could let you down, as on subsiding cliffs! But as rocks were just there, permanently (usually), there were no problems to solve. It wasn't until the eighteenth century when people like James Hutton began to look at rocks more closely that the realisation came that rocks hadn't in fact been 'there' for ever, but had been formed by a variety of processes. Some of the processes involved heat and pressure deep within the Earth, but others could be seen by anybody with open eyes because they act where we live today, at the surface of the Earth. In fact, it was soon realised that if you study rocks carefully enough, you can actually work out how they formed – that is, if you become a rock detective, you can work out what happened and why.

The Evidence

A good rock detective works in exactly the same way as a police detective. The rock detective realises that there is a problem to solve (i.e. how did the rock form?); the police detective has a crime to solve. Both go first to the scene of the 'crime'. At the rock face the rock detective should begin by standing back and surveying the scene to see the general pattern, recording his observations in a notebook. He must try to see what is 'normal' and pick out any strange or unusual points. Then he must examine the evidence more closely, because often it is the finest detail that will give him the solution. This fine detail can be gained only by accurate and detailed observation, using a magnifying glass if necessary, and by careful measurement and collection of specimens for later analysis. Everything important should be recorded in notes, drawings, photographs, etc. No clue is too small, or too large, to be unimportant, because an answer that does not fit all the evidence is a wrong answer.

Back at the Lab

In the lab the problem should be approached in two ways. First, all the samples brought in should be tested. What are they made of? What gives them their colour, size, shape, etc.? Can a microscope, chemical testing or 'modern technology' help to answer these questions?

Second, we can do experiments to help answer some of the questions. A forensic scientist can conduct an experiment to find out if a brown stain on parchment could have been formed by blood, by dropping blood on to parchment in a variety of ways and observing the results. Likewise a rock scientist can attempt to find out how rippled sandstones formed by flowing water over sand in different ways to see if the same types of ripples can be produced. Both scientists can do physical, chemical and biological experiments to add to the evidence required.

Recreating the Scene of the Crime

What was it like when the rock was formed? What was it like when the crime was committed? The police detective might try to recreate the scene by choosing the correct day and time, by using actors and dressing them up, by providing cars or other equipment, and so on. The rock detective cannot do this in the same way because he can't recreate a delta or a desert environment near the coastal cliffs that he is examining. Instead, he 'recreates' the scene by visiting places on Earth where those conditions occur today.

Once there, he has to examine the environment carefully for all the clues it provides. He must observe what types of sediment are there and note the patterns they make. He must observe, measure and record the processes acting in the environment to lay the sediments down. These could involve the moving of sediment in a physical way by wind, water, etc., or chemical changes, or the influences of the vegetation and the animals living there. The rock detective must study the distribution of all these factors and how they work in space and time. In short, he must study the ways in which the physics, chemistry, biology and geography of the environment interact to produce the geological sequences of sediments preserved.

Armed with these extra clues from 'recreating the scene of the crime', both the police and the rock scientist can then begin to make a case, to suggest a solution to the problem.

The Case

Both kinds of detective prepare their case by assembling all the evidence they have amassed from broad and detailed examination of the ancient rock (or the scene of the crime), from lab testing and experimentation, and from modern environments where sediments are being formed and laid down today (recreating the scene). They will also examine the published work of other scientists for more information and may gain important clues from studying these 'previous cases'. When suggesting their solutions to the problem, they put forward hypotheses backed by all the evidence that they think is relevant. This is the 'case' that can then face 'trial'.

The Trial and Conviction

In all trials the prosecution, on behalf of the detective, has to convince the court that his interpretation of the evidence is correct by providing honestly all the evidence that is available to support his case. Instead of convincing the legal experts, the court and the jury, the rock detective has to convince scientists who are geological experts. As in all trials, one flaw in the evidence will bring his case down; one important question that cannot be answered correctly will make his interpretation suspect. But, if the case does stand up, if the evidence and its interpretation are convincing, he will win a conviction, the conviction of all the experts that he is correct. He will have won his case.

Unlike a police detective who cannot return to court, if the rock detective 'loses his case' he does have a second chance. He can look again at the evidence, he can gather more evidence, particularly where he had problems with his 'case' before, and finally, when he is satisfied, he can present a new case. He can't afford to 'lose' too often, though, or he will lose his reputation too!

Why Be a Detective?

The aim of the detective is to find out the truth from all the evidence available. The police detective can use this information to have the guilty convicted and to allow the innocent to go free. Why does the rock detective need to get at the truth?

The 'truth' to the rock detective is a better understanding of the natural world we live in, both now and as it was in the geological past. He can develop an understanding of the geography and ecology of the world today into an understanding of the palaeogeography and palaeoecology of the Earth in times past with the physical, chemical and biological processes active then. These studies can help to explain why some rocks are soft, others hard, why some collapse and others don't, and where buildings, motorways and dams should or should not be built today. They can show where the best building stones, oil reserves, underground water supplies, or reserves of copper, gold or coal can be found.

The truth to a police detective helps to build up a knowledge of people and how they react in certain situations, which can be used to predict and analyse future events. The truth to a rock detective helps us to understand how the Earth worked in the past, how it works today and how it is likely to work and change in the future.

The Rock Detective in these Chapters

We shall begin this book by looking at the evidence. Some of the evidence is happening outside our windows today. By examining this, and by asking and answering the questions at the end of each chapter, you will ensure that you understand what is going on and what effects are being produced. You will also be asked to consider the evidence gained from testing and investigation in the lab, and the ways in which field studies can contribute to our knowledge. These considerations will give you further important insights into the 'cases' being studied.

In Book 2, you will be asked to 'recreate the scene of the crime' by analysing the many different environments in which sediment is being deposited on Earth today. The investigations and questions presented there will build and test your understanding of this part of the study too.

Armed with this knowledge and understanding you too will be able to examine a cliff face of sedimentary rock and do the 'rock detective' job yourself. If you do it correctly, you will be able to show how the Earth worked in the past, how it works today and how it is likely to develop. By applying the information given in Books 1 and 2 on the background to economic geology in sedimentary rocks, you will be able to use your new understanding to help in the search for the raw materials that are the basis of the progress and development of mankind.

Practical Investigation and Fieldwork

1. What is the scientific problem?
Pick up a rock, any natural rock from a beach, a hillside, a ruined wall or even from your own garden. Write down any scientific problems you can find in it. These may involve testing, experimentation, 'recreating the scene of the crime' or considering the use of the rock in today's world.

Repeat this exercise for:

a) rocks used in buildings, shop fronts, gravestones, roads and paths, etc.;
b) man-made 'rocks' such as bricks, concrete, etc.;
c) rocks in exposures such as cliffs, quarries and road cuttings.

2. How can the problem be solved?
The early scientists had to solve the problems of rocks without any background knowledge. In fact, they were in the same state as you are at the beginning of your studies. So have a go, like they did. Work out and write down how you would solve the problems which you identified in the investigations above. Think about what you would do if your ideas didn't work. How would you gather new evidence, modify your experiments, etc., to make out a new 'case'?

Test Your Understanding

1. Look at the diagrams of rocks in this book. Try to work out how they formed. Decide on the types of investigation you could carry out to test your ideas.

2. List the ways in which studies of sedimentary rocks can be useful to us. This will involve considering the ways in which resources from the Earth contribute to economic and technological growth (in both developed and developing countries), to society in general, and to the well-being of you, your family and your friends.

2. MAKING AND MOVING SEDIMENT

The Sedimentary Cycle

Loose sediment at the Earth's surface is picked up by moving currents of wind and water and is carried along until they slow down, when the sediment is deposited. Over long periods of time the sediment layers can build up into thick **sedimentary sequences**. The buried layers, under the pressure of the layers above and the higher temperatures that are present beneath the Earth's surface, become sedimentary rocks. Movements of the Earth's crust can cause these sedimentary rocks to become uplifted and exposed to attack by the weather. Particles then become loosened and broken down to become available as sediment for a new sedimentary cycle.

This is the sedimentary cycle in its simplest form. The movement of sediment in this fashion was first recognised by James Hutton in his book *Theory of the Earth*, published in 1788. We now recognise that the sedimentary cycle is part of a series of cycles that have produced the shape and character of the Earth's crust. Figure 2.1 shows these cycles diagrammatically. The arrows on the diagram indicate processes which cause change. The products of these processes are shown in boxes. We can understand the different types of rock that make up the crust of the Earth only by studying the processes by which those rocks are formed.

The Formation of Sediment

Sediment is formed in several different ways, eventually producing a variety of different sediment bodies and rock types. By far the majority of sediment (about 85 per cent) is produced by the weathering and erosion of existing rocks. This sediment, once transported and deposited, is called **clastic** sediment (from the Greek *klastos* – broken) or **detrital** sediment (detritus is material produced by wearing down). It ranges in size from boulders and coarse gravels, through sands and silts to fine muds. This sediment is deposited mainly by physical processes. Material thrown out by volcanoes, called **pyroclastic** material, is also sediment formed by physical processes.

Biological processes are also important in the formation of sediment. Many animals in the sea build their shells and skeletons by removing the charged particles or ions that make up calcium carbonate ($CaCO_3$) or silica (SiO_2) from the sea water and precipitating them to form solid skeletal material that can be preserved. The organic material of plants can also be preserved. These accumulations are called **biogenic** sediments.

If these sediments are moved by currents or waves then their characteristics are due partly to their biogenic origin, and partly to the processes of transportation. Beach sands of broken shells are formed in this way and this type of sedimentation is known as **bioclastic** sedimentation.

Figure 2.1
The sedimentary cycle and other Earth cycles.
Processes are shown as arrows, the products of the processes in boxes. The close links between the sedimentary cycle and other Earth cycles are shown. Write a brief description of one of the products formed by each of the processes shown on the diagram.

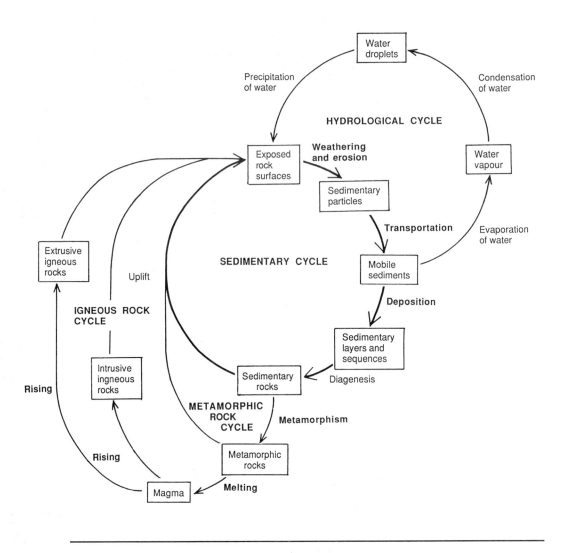

Sediments are also formed by chemical processes such as precipitation by the evaporation of sea water. Under tropical conditions sea water evaporates and this causes fine crystals of calcium carbonate to form and become deposited as lime mud. Other evaporite minerals can also form, such as gypsum ($CaSO_4.2H_2O$) and halite ($NaCl$). Strong evaporation of sea water where the water is being agitated by currents or waves can cause carbonate precipitation of small spherical particles called **ooids**, producing oolitic sands.

These examples illustrate some of the main processes by which sediments are formed. The processes and products of sediment formation are summarised in Figure 2.2. This figure also shows the close links between physical, biological and chemical processes. The rest of this chapter is concerned with the three most important and widespread sediment formation processes: weathering, erosion and transportation.

Figure 2.2
A classification of sediments based on their processes of formation.
Where would the following rock types be found in this classification: oolithic ironstone, bauxite deposits, fossil screes, pelleted limestone (pellets made by organisms eating and excreting lime mud), stromatolites (growths of algae which trap lime mud)?

Main Process of Formation		Sediment Group	Sediment	Rock Equivalent
Physical	Transported materials	Clastic	Boulders and gravel Sands Silts Muds	Conglomerate Sandstone Siltstone Mudstone
	Volcanic	Pyroclastic	Bombs and lapilli Ash	Agglomerate Tuff
— — —	Transported biological materials	Bioclastic	Reef talus Shell sands	Bioclastic limestone Bioclastic limestone
Biological	Formed by organisms	Biogenic	Reefs Oozes formed from micro-organisms Accumulations of plant material	Biogenic limestone Biogenic limestone or chert Coal
— — —	Formed by organic and chemical processes	Soil	Soils	Palaeosol (including calcrete, etc.)
Chemical	Precipitation by evaporation	Chemical precipitate	Lime mud Evaporites	Micrite (fine-grained limestone) Evaporite deposit
— — — Physical	Evaporation and agitation of water	Oolites	Ooid sands	Oolitic limestone

Weathering and Mineral Stability

Weathering may be defined as the *in situ* (in place) break-up and breakdown (or decay) of rock at the Earth's surface. It occurs because all rocks were formed under conditions of higher pressure and temperature and lower humidity than those found at the Earth's surface. They are therefore unstable at the Earth's surface and become changed into new minerals and sediments that are more stable.

Weathering and **erosion** are very closely linked to one another but they should not be confused. In weathering there is no movement of solid material away from the weathered area although crystals may expand and contract and water containing dissolved minerals may pass through. Any movement of solid material is regarded as erosion; this is dealt with later in this chapter.

In 1938 Goldich made a careful investigation of weathered igneous rocks in order to put the major rock-forming minerals into an order of stability. The mineral sequence he produced ranges from the least stable (olivine and calcium-rich plagioclase) to the most stable (quartz). Since then other investigators working in different areas and climates have shown his sequence to be correct (see Figure 2.3). This sequence is exactly the same as the sequence in which minerals crystallise from a cooling silicate magma, as shown by Bowen (1928) and now known as Bowen's Reaction Series. The series shows that the minerals which crystallise first at the highest temperatures are olivine and calcium-rich plagioclase and the last mineral to crystallise is quartz. Thus the high temperature minerals are less stable at the surface of the Earth than the low temperature minerals, olivine breaking down before pyroxene, etc.

7

Figure 2.3
The order of stability of the common rock-forming silicate minerals (the same as Bowen's Reaction Series).
Find out the chemical formulae of the minerals shown and calculate the ratio of silicon to oxygen. Which are the more stable at the Earth's surface, minerals with a lot of silicon or those with little silicon in relation to oxygen?

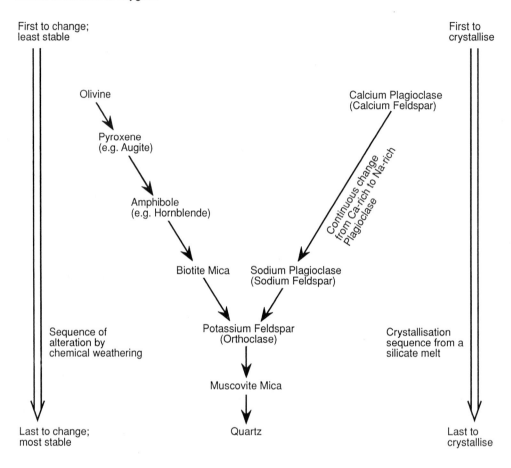

Weathering Processes

The processes of weathering can be subdivided into chemical, physical and biological. However, this subdivision is rather artificial because the different types of process are so closely related to one another that it may be difficult to decide whether a process is mainly chemical, physical or biological. For example, the chemical addition of water to mineral lattices causes the physical effect of expansion and possibly rock break-up. This process could be classified as either chemical or physical. However, despite these problems, it is useful to classify weathering processes into the three groups in order to describe and discuss them.

Chemical Weathering
Minerals which are unstable at the surface of the Earth become broken down by the processes of **chemical weathering** into minerals which are more stable and thus more closely in equilibrium with the surface conditions.

Chemical weathering breaks down the minerals into two main constituents, the **solutes** which dissolve in water, and the **residuum** of original and new minerals, which is insoluble. The new minerals produced, usually clays, have a greater volume and lower density than the original minerals. The solutes are atoms or molecules which have been separated from the parent minerals by the weathering process in the form of ions, such as Ca^{2+} (calcium ion) and SO_4^{2-} (sulphate ion). The main ions involved in weathering processes are shown in Figure 2.4. The ions become dissolved in the water present in

Figure 2.4
Major ions involved in weathering and soil formation.
Use the table to list three chemical compounds that would be very unstable and would dissolve easily (such as sodium hydrogen carbonate, $NaHCO_3$) and three chemical compounds that would be very stable (such as quartz, silicon dioxide, SiO_2).

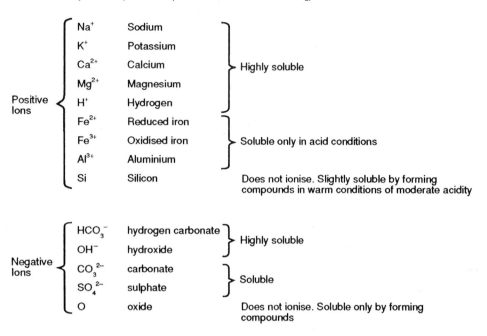

the pores of the rock and are usually carried away from the area in pore water flow. They remain in solution until a change occurs (e.g. by evaporation of the water or by biological activity) which produces a chemical combination. For example:

$$Ca^{2+} + SO_4^{2-} + 2H_2O \rightarrow CaSO_4.2H_2O$$
$$\text{water} \qquad \text{gypsum}$$

The role of the solution process is vital in all types of chemical weathering because, by removing the ions in solution, fresh mineral surfaces are exposed to chemical attack. The major chemical weathering reactions are described below:

Carbonation

Water falling through the atmosphere as rain absorbs carbon dioxide (CO_2). It absorbs a great deal more CO_2 as it passes as pore water through the soil. The CO_2 reacts with the water to form weak carbonic acid.

$$H_2O + CO_2 \rightarrow H_2CO_3$$
$$\text{carbonic acid}$$

The carbonic acid attacks calcium carbonate minerals (calcite and aragonite) forming calcium hydrogen carbonate.

$$H_2CO_3 + CaCO_3 \rightarrow Ca^{2+} + 2HCO_3^-$$

As the chemical equation shows, the calcium hydrogen carbonate produced is in the form of ions which are soluble in water. The pore waters dissolve this calcium hydrogen carbonate and carry it away from the weathered surface.

Carbonation is most important in the breakdown of carbonate rocks such as limestone. The characteristic features of limestone scenery are formed in this way and areas with this type of scenery are called **karst** regions. **Dissolution** (or dissolving) of limestone by carbonation leaves behind a residuum of insoluble minerals such as clays and since limestone surfaces are lowered by weathering, a surface blanket of clay often remains.

The Cretaceous chalk rocks (of which the White Cliffs of Dover are formed) often have a surface deposit of 'clay with flints' formed in this way.

Water from limestone areas contains a high proportion of ions in solution and is called **hard water**. Soap does not lather easily in hard water and when hard water is boiled, the carbonation reaction is reversed and a precipitate of white calcium carbonate is deposited as 'fur' in kettles and hot water pipes.

Carbonation is also important in the chemical attack on silicate minerals because when carbon dioxide is dissolved in the water, hydrogen ions (H^+) are readily available and this speeds up the hydrolysis reaction on silicates (as described in the next section). Even so, the hydrolysis reaction on the silicates is usually much slower than the carbonation reaction on carbonates.

Note that the carbonation reaction should not be confused with the similar-sounding process of carbonisation. **Carbonisation** is the conversion of organic material to carbon by the loss of the volatile constituents (e.g. natural gas). Coal is formed in this way.

Hydrolysis

The reaction of a mineral with water causing breakdown of the original mineral structure is called **hydrolysis**. It is the most important chemical reaction affecting silicate minerals. It attacks feldspars and since these are the most common minerals at the Earth's surface, hydrolysis is probably one of the most widespread inorganic chemical reactions on Earth.

The reaction of water with olivine is a simple breakdown.

$$MgFeSiO_4 + 4H_2O \rightarrow Mg^{2+} + Fe^{2+} + 4OH^- + H_4SiO_4$$

olivine   water   ions in solution   silicic acid in solution

If enough pore water is present, all the products can be carried away in solution. More commonly there is insufficient water for this reaction to occur and instead the olivine alters to serpentine, releasing iron.

The hydrolysis reaction of water with feldspars is similar, if more complex, because carbonation plays a critical role in releasing hydrogen ions for reaction with the feldspar.

$$2KAlSi_3O_8 + 11H_2O + 2CO_2 \rightarrow Al_2Si_2O_5(OH)_4 + 4H_4SiO_4 + 2K^+ + 2HCO_3^-$$

potassium feldspar, orthoclase   water   carbon dioxide   clay mineral, kaolinite   silicic acid in solution   potassium and hydrogen carbonate ions in solution

Calcium- and sodium-rich feldspars react in a similar way to form a clay mineral residuum. The dissolved silica and calcium, sodium, potassium and hydrogen carbonate ions are carried away in solution. The clays formed by hydrolysis contain little water but these water-poor clays frequently become hydrated to water-rich clays by the addition of water molecules.

Hydration

Hydration is the addition of water molecules to the atomic structure of a mineral and so differs from the hydrolysis process where the water causes chemical breakdown. A simple example of hydration is the formation of gypsum from anhydrite.

$$CaSO_4 + 2H_2O \rightarrow CaSO_4.2H_2O$$

anhydrite   water   gypsum

The addition of the water molecules gives gypsum a lower density and a larger volume than the original anhydrite. The expansion has the physical effect of assisting rock break-up.

Oxidation

The chemical process of oxidation affects many types of mineral but is particularly effective on those minerals containing iron. Iron can exist naturally in two states, either as iron ions with two charges (Fe^{2+}) which form greenish compounds, or as ions with three charges (Fe^{3+}) which form red, yellow and brownish compounds. When Fe^{2+} compounds react with oxygen they change to Fe^{3+} compounds and this process is called **oxidation**. Most rocks contain iron minerals in small quantities and weathering of these by oxidation produces either reddish hematite (Fe_2O_3) or yellowish-brown minerals like limonite ($2Fe_2O_3.3H_2O$). These minerals form surface coatings on the majority of rock surfaces exposed to the atmosphere and often hide the true colour of the rock. Freshly-broken surfaces of Cretaceous Greensands are green due to the presence of the green mineral glauconite but, on contact with the atmosphere, the glauconite generally oxidises to yellowish-brown limonite, altering the surface colour of the rock. In igneous rocks, the iron present in the common ferromagnesian minerals (olivine, pyroxene, amphibole and biotite) is nearly always oxidised to Fe^{3+} iron. This, together with the weathered magnetite, is responsible for the colour changes seen on the surfaces of most weathered igneous rocks.

Most surface environments are oxidising or oxic. The opposite reducing or **anoxic** conditions are much less common. They do occur when rotting organic material removes the oxygen from an environment, such as in a swamp. Under these stinking, unpleasant conditions Fe^{3+} iron is reduced to Fe^{2+} iron and sometimes crystals of pyrite (FeS_2) can be precipitated.

Ion exchange

Some positive ions are more attractive to certain mineral structures than others. When pore waters rich in an attractive ion are in contact with such a mineral, the ions are exchanged. This often expands or contracts the mineral structure, thus causing a physical weathering effect on the surrounding minerals. For example, sodium-rich clay minerals can react with calcium-rich pore waters, exchanging sodium for calcium, which causes shrinking. A similar reaction is used as the basis of commercial water softeners where the hard water containing dissolved salts such as calcium hydrogen carbonate ($Ca(HCO_3)_2$) passes through minerals rich in sodium. The ions exchange so that the minerals become rich in calcium and the dissolved salt becomes sodium hydrogen carbonate ($NaHCO_3$) which has none of the effects of hard water.

Chelation

The term **chelation** comes from the word 'chelate' meaning 'claw-like' and it nicely describes the process by which organic compounds dissolved in pore waters can claw on to and remove metal ions, holding them within their atomic structures. Because the organic compounds effectively remove the metal ions from the water, by binding them inside their atomic structures, the water is able to dissolve more metal ions from the mineral under attack. The organic compounds containing the metal ions are eventually removed from the area by pore water flow. Chelation is most effective when thick layers of rotting organic humus in the soil supply the pore waters with organic compounds.

The effects of chemical weathering on the major rock-forming minerals are summarised in Figure 2.5 which shows that the end products of most weathering processes are clay and oxidised iron minerals and that pore waters rich in dissolved silica and dissolved ions (e.g. Na^+, Ca^{2+}, HCO_3^-, etc.) are produced in the process. Quartz is released by the decay of the surrounding minerals, frequently adding quartz sand to the residuum.

Physical Weathering

Physical weathering is the mechanical break-up of rock and mineral particles into smaller fragments. Physical and chemical processes are very closely linked; some chemical processes produce mechanical effects and all physical weathering is helped by the chemical breakdown of the minerals involved. The main significance of physical weathering is that each newly-formed fracture provides two new surfaces open for chemical attack.

Figure 2.5
Weathering products of the major rock-forming minerals.
A basalt contains minerals from the top of Bowen's Reaction Series. What are the weathering products of a basalt?

MINERAL	WEATHERING PRODUCTS				
	Serpentine	Clay Minerals	Oxidised iron minerals	Dissolved silica	Dissolved salts
Olivine	✓	—	✓	✓	✓
Pyroxene	—	✓	✓	✓	✓
Amphibole	—	✓	✓	✓	✓
Mica	—	✓	✓ if iron is present	✓	✓
Feldspar	—	✓	—	✓	✓
Calcite	—	—	—	—	✓
Quartz	Weathered only in extreme conditions				

The breaking or brittle failure of the rock is the result of stress which may be caused in several ways. Where the stress is applied at intervals, rock fatigue (similar to metal fatigue) may be a significant factor, but few investigations have been carried out on this difficult topic.

Insolation

Insolation is the effect on rocks of heat from the sun. When days are very warm and nights very cold, as in desert regions, stress is produced in rocks by the great temperature changes. The evidence for this is the 'gunshot sounds' frequently heard in deserts at night and the angular 'spalled' fragments found beneath rock faces in desert regions. When dry rocks are subjected to repeated heating and cooling in the lab to investigate the effects of insolation very little happens. This probably shows that the presence of at least small quantities of water is vital (e.g. the dew in deserts). Since different minerals expand at different rates, insolation has more effect on rocks containing several minerals than on monomineralic rocks.

Wetting and drying

Several clay minerals swell when they absorb water through hydration and shrink when the water is lost. Thus repeated wetting and drying causes repeated expansion and contraction and eventually failure, or break-up, of the rocks that contain the clay minerals.

Freezing and thawing

Freezing and thawing is most effective in periglacial and mountain areas where freezing occurs at night and thawing in the daytime. When water freezes, it increases in volume by 9 per cent (it is one of the very few natural substances that does expand and become less dense in changing from the liquid to the solid state). Any fracture filled with water will be slightly prised apart when the water freezes, and on thawing the water will penetrate further into the fracture. This process repeats itself and eventually produces angular fragments of rock debris of many different sizes.

Crystallisation of minerals

When water evaporates from fractures in rocks, the dissolved minerals are precipitated. In some cases the forces of crystallisation are so strong that the rock is split. For example, the forceful crystallisation of halite (NaCl) in desert and coastal areas is a very effective mechanical weathering agent. In urban and industrial areas rainwater polluted by sulphur dioxide (SO_2) reacts with calcium carbonate ($CaCO_3$) to form gypsum ($CaSO_4.2H_2O$). This also crystallises forcefully, causing the fracture and failure of building stones. These crystallisation processes demonstrate the very close links between physical and chemical weathering.

Chemical reactions causing volume changes

Most chemical weathering produces new minerals of greater volume. These have the mechanical effect of forcing rock apart. This process again illustrates the close links between physical and chemical weathering.

Stress release

When rock sequences are deeply buried they contract due to the great **overburden pressure** from the layers of rock above. On being exposed at the surface they expand and fractures form parallel to the surface. These near-horizontal parallel joints are called **stress release** joints (i.e. caused by the stress of the overburden pressure having been released) and can often be seen near the tops of quarry walls. Stress release is probably the main cause of the **exfoliation** seen in granite terrains. This is the peeling off of large curved sheets or slabs from the surface of an exposed rock face. In areas near the tropics, steep-sided, dome-shaped outcrops called **inselbergs** are formed by exfoliation. Stress release jointing is also important in the formation of **tors** of granite and massive sandstone in temperate regions.

Plants

Plants cause mechanical weathering effects when their roots widen cracks beneath the surface. In windy conditions large plants have important levering effects and can bring down blocks from cliffs and garden walls. Fallen trees turn up soil and sometimes provide valuable exposures of bedrock.

Biological Effects

Plants have been effective agents of weathering since they began colonising the land surface in Silurian times. They do cause mechanical effects but the most important role of organic material is biochemical, as illustrated by the chelation process. Not only do plants supply the organic material for chelation and most of the carbon dioxide involved in carbonation and hydrolysis, but they also remove from minerals the ions they need for growth. Experiments have shown that primitive plants such as lichens are particularly effective in removing these ions causing mineral and rock breakdown. This is why lichens are the first plants to grow on bare rock surfaces.

Bacteria play a vital role in mineral breakdown and soil-forming processes and, in experiments, feldspars and micas have been shown to decompose twice as fast when bacteria are present. Other soil organisms have important effects as well and it is probably true that much weathering of rocks is caused ultimately by organic processes.

Controls on Weathering

Mineral Stability

Rocks that contain a high percentage of minerals that are unstable at the Earth's surface decay faster than rocks with a low percentage of unstable minerals. Thus, on the basis of mineral stability, gabbro – which contains minerals near the top of Bowen's Reaction Series, such as pyroxene and calcium-rich plagioclase – will weather faster than granite, which contains minerals near the bottom of the series, such as quartz and potassium feldspar.

Sedimentary rocks formed from sediments that have undergone long distances of transport will have lost their unstable minerals during transportation. These **mature** sediments are more stable than **immature** sediments, which have only been transported short distances. Sediments that have undergone several sedimentary cycles of erosion, transportation, deposition, rock formation, uplift, erosion, etc. (see Figure 2.1) are very stable and very mature. These are known as **polycyclic** sediments.

Crystal Size in Igneous Rocks

Fine-grained igneous rocks such as basalt have large numbers of mineral surfaces open to attack by chemical weathering. In some circumstances, therefore, they break down faster than their coarse-grained equivalents – in this case, gabbro. However, coarse-grained igneous rocks allow water to penetrate deeper into the rock along crystal junctions and so in some cases can decay faster than similar fine-grained rocks.

Particle Size in Sedimentary Rocks

Fine-grained clastic rocks have small pore spaces allowing water to penetrate only slowly, so that weathering rates are slow. Coarse-grained clastic rocks allow fast water percolation and faster weathering unless the pore spaces have become filled with cement during the rock-forming processes. Silica cements are more resistant to weathering than carbonate, iron and other types of cement.

Figure 2.6
The increase in surface area caused by fracturing.
As a block breaks into smaller blocks, the surface area increases while the volume stays the same. The increased surface area makes more surface available to chemical weathering. Calculate the surface area if each of the eight newly-formed blocks were divided into four.

Single boulder, approximately 1 metre cubed
Volume = 1 cubic metre
Surface area = 6 square metres

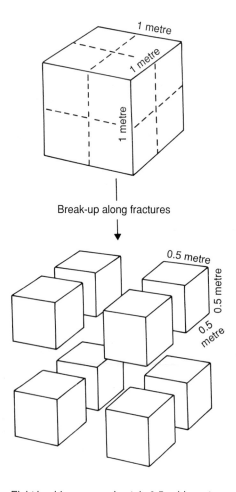

Break-up along fractures

Eight boulders, approximately 0.5 cubic metre
Volume = 1 cubic metre
Surface area = 12 square metres

Rock Weaknesses

Weaknesses are formed either during the formation of the rock, in which case they are called primary structures (e.g. bedding), or later, in which case they are called secondary structures (e.g. joints and faults). The greater the surface area of rock open to weathering through the weaknesses, the faster the weathering will be. Every fracture present in the rock allows water to attack the minerals on both sides of the fracture, increasing the weathering rate, as shown in Figure 2.6. Bedding is the most common weakness in sedimentary rocks and the penetration of water along bedding planes is faster where the frayed edge of dipping rocks is open to the atmosphere. Jointing is the critical weakness in most igneous rocks and some sedimentary rocks, particularly limestones. In limestone areas, limestone pavements can be created on horizontal or nearly horizontal bedding planes (as shown in Figure 2.7) and extensive cave and pothole systems are formed in thick limestone sequences (Figure 2.8). In cave systems that have been abandoned by fast-flowing waters, water which is rich in dissolved calcium hydrogen carbonate, as it drips into caves, can form stalagmites, stalactites and other beautiful formations by the slight evaporation of the water and precipitation of calcium carbonate. In metamorphic rocks, cleavage and foliation are the main weaknesses attacked by weathering.

The Harshness of the Chemical Environment

Chemical weathering is far more important than physical weathering in general and so the major control on the rates of weathering over broad areas of the Earth is the effectiveness of pore waters in attacking minerals. Where there is little pore water, or where pore water is frozen, chemical attack is very limited. Where pore water is abundant, temperature is very important since most chemical reactions speed up at higher temperatures.

Figure 2.7
The formation of limestone pavements by chemical weathering.
Water, rich in carbon dioxide from the air and soil, flows down the joints causing carbonation and solution. The joints are steadily widened to form grykes, leaving the upstanding clints which are obvious when the soil has been removed by glacial erosion. Why is the initial soil cover necessary for a limestone pavement to develop?

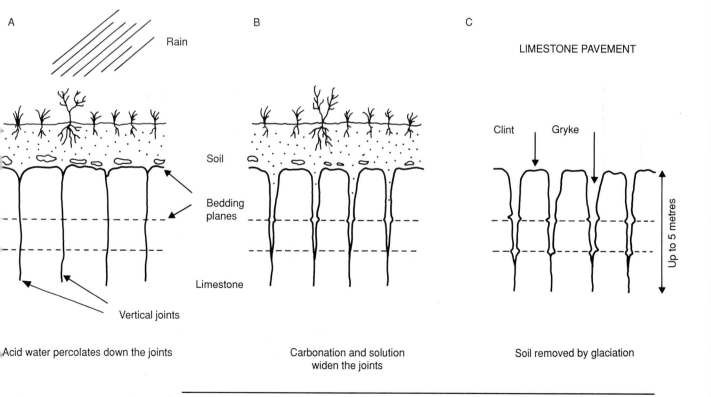

A

Rain

Soil

Bedding planes

Limestone

Vertical joints

Acid water percolates down the joints

B

Carbonation and solution widen the joints

C

LIMESTONE PAVEMENT

Clint   Gryke

Up to 5 metres

Soil removed by glaciation

Figure 2.8
The formation of limestone cave systems.
Why do cave systems formed above the water table differ from those formed below the water table?

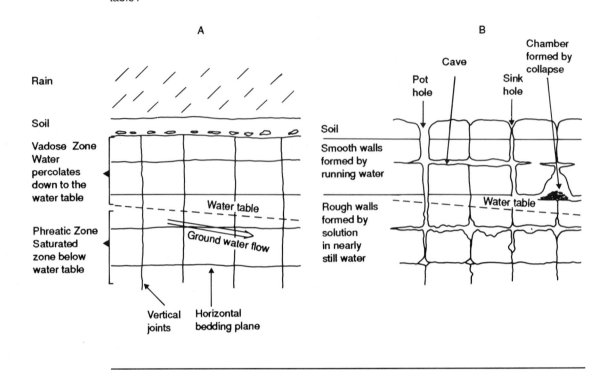

In Arctic regions where there is little water available and where the water that is present is either very cold or is locked up as ice, chemical weathering has little effect. The main weathering process which affects exposed rock surfaces is thus freeze-thaw, causing the mechanical breakage of the rock.

Chemical weathering is much more active in temperate regions like Britain, where much more water is available, temperatures are warmer and vegetation cover is extensive. Soils of varying thickness, usually rich in clay, are produced on the rounded and subdued topography. In upland areas of more resistant bedrock, freeze-thaw weathering is effective in the winter, producing steep rock faces and scree slopes.

In tropical humid regions of high temperatures and heavy rainfall with thick vegetation cover, chemical weathering is very active. Under these conditions, clays decompose and silica can be dissolved and carried away in solution. Soils are produced which are rich in residual iron and aluminium minerals. Very thick weathering profiles can be produced with soils up to 100 metres thick forming at times. Physical weathering effects are minimal due to the vegetation cover.

In arid and semi-arid areas such as deserts and savannah regions, there is little water available and so chemical weathering effects are limited. Soils are generally thin and poor and the main form of weathering is by insolation. The alternate heating and cooling from day to night, aided by the small quantities of water which condense at night as dew, cause the break-up of exposed rock surfaces into angular fragments. Rocks such as limestone and sandstone which contain only one type of mineral (i.e. **monomineralic** rocks) are most resistant under these conditions and so form the areas of higher land.

Relief
In areas of steep slopes, weathered material is quickly removed by erosion exposing new materials to weathering. In areas of subdued relief, weathering rates are slower and chemical weathering predominates: thus thick weathering profiles can form under these conditions.

Regolith and Soil Formation

The blanket of loose weathered material that covers most bedrock surfaces is called **regolith**. The regolith is formed *in situ* from the resistant minerals such as quartz and the newly-formed minerals such as clay minerals. When vegetation is present, the regolith is subjected to the processes that form soil.

Soil formation is a biochemical process that occurs only beneath a cover of vegetation. Thus no soils are formed where vegetation is absent, such as in polar or very arid conditions. Soil formation was not possible before vegetation colonised the land in the late Silurian and ancient soils are first widely recognised in Devonian sedimentary rocks.

The study of modern soils is called **pedology** and is important not only to geologists but also to geographers, farmers, engineers, etc. Soil scientists or pedologists study soil by examining **soil profiles**, that is, the changes in the soil from the bedrock up to the ground surface. Soil profiles are examined either in natural exposures by digging pits, or by taking soil cores. Soil thicknesses can vary between a few millimetres and tens of metres, depending upon the soil-forming conditions.

Most soils are layered and these layers, which are parallel to the land surface, are called **horizons**. Pedologists identify a great number of different horizons, but in most soils three major horizons can be recognised: the A, B and C horizons, shown in Figure 2.9. These three horizons can vary greatly in thickness, from up to 20 metres to being totally absent.

The A horizon is usually dark in colour, being rich in decayed vegetation called **humus**. After rain, water infiltrates through the A horizon, dissolving all the soluble minerals and carrying down the fine-grained clay minerals. This process of solution and clay mineral removal is known as **leaching**.

Figure 2.9
A typical soil profile.
What happens to the soluble minerals that do not become deposited in the B horizon?

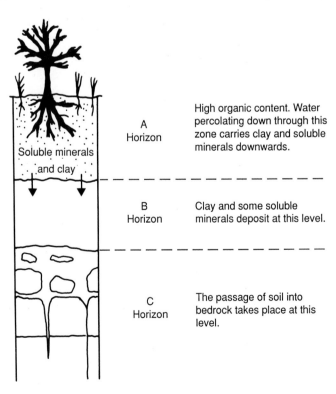

Leaching carries the dissolved minerals and clays down to the B horizon where the clays become deposited, filling up and blocking the pore spaces. Some of the dissolved salts also precipitate out of solution in the B horizon.

The C horizon is where the change from soil to bedrock takes place and this is usually a gradual change from obvious soil, through rotted and weathered bedrock to the unaltered parent rock material.

The five principal factors affecting soil formation are: parent rock type; climate; vegetation; slope; time. Time is critical as soils develop only slowly. Newly-formed soils are **immature**; soils that have developed over long periods of time are **mature** soils. If enough time is available the parent material will decay until it reaches near equilibrium with the climate and associated vegetation. Mature soil types are to a large extent, therefore, controlled by climate. To exemplify the major soil-forming processes linked to climatic types, the formation of three different soil types is described below. The simplified distribution of these three types, podzols, iron-rich tropical soils and calcic soils, is shown in Figure 2.10.

Figure 2.10
The world distribution of three major soil types.
What controls the distribution of these three types of soil?

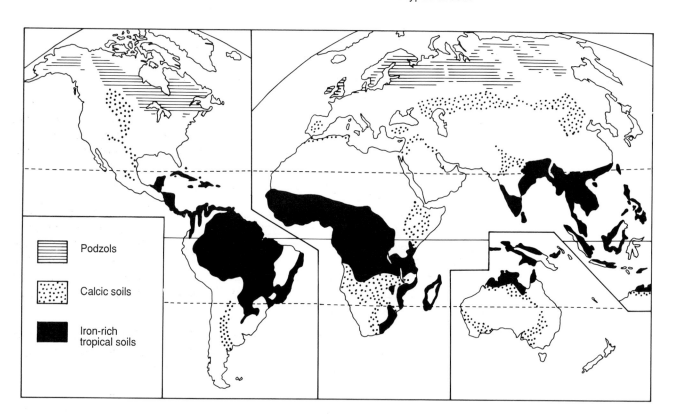

Podzols

Podzols are formed in cool temperate climatic regions with moderate rainfall where the vegetation produces very acid organic material. These conditions are typically found in the coniferous forests and heathlands of upland Britain. Podzols are formed by the process known as podzolisation and are known as spodosols in the soil classification now generally used (American Soil Survey, 7th Approximation, 1960). Podzol formation is shown in Figure 2.11. The acid rainwater breaks down the clay minerals of the A horizon and dissolves all the products of this breakdown, with the

Figure 2.11
The formation of podzols.
Why is silica not removed from the A horizon in solution?

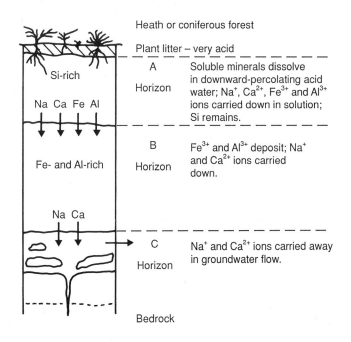

exception of silica, so that the A horizon becomes enriched in silica. In the B horizon, the iron and aluminium ions are deposited, largely as oxides, forming an iron- and aluminium-rich layer. The remaining dissolved ions are carried through the C horizon and away in the groundwater.

Iron-rich Tropical Soils

These are formed in tropical humid regions such as areas of equatorial rain forest, found in central Africa, and monsoon forest, found in South-East Asia (Figure 2.12). They are classified as **oxisols**. Under the hot conditions of high rainfall with thick vegetation cover, chemical weathering is intense and silica is slightly soluble. The silica is leached from the A horizon together with other soluble ions, leaving it enriched in iron and aluminium. Some clay forms in the B horizon but most of the soluble ions are swept through the C horizon and away with the groundwater.

In western Scotland **palaeosols** (i.e. fossil soils) that were rich in iron formed on some of the extensive lava flows that were extruded during the mid-Tertiary period. These indicate that the climate must have been at least sub-tropical at the time.

In monsoonal and savannah areas today where there are marked wet and dry seasons, a layer greatly enriched in iron and aluminium can form near the base of the A horizon. This is a red-brown earthy material which can harden rapidly when exposed to the atmosphere and is known as **laterite** (from the Latin *later* – a brick). If laterites are exposed to the atmosphere by erosion of the soil above, they form solid crusts of iron-rich material which are resistant to weathering, and largely infertile. These **duricrusts** now cover large areas of semi-arid Australia and similar regions of the world. In Kampuchea (Cambodia) fresh soft laterite was cut, dried and allowed to harden before being used to build the famous Angkor Wat temples.

Calcic Soils

These soils form in semi-arid grassland areas and so are included in the **aridisols** section of the soil classification system. One of the processes which form calcic soils is shown in Figure 2.13. In the semi-arid regions where evaporation is greater than

Figure 2.12
The formation of iron-rich tropical soils.
How can this process form aluminium ore under certain circumstances?

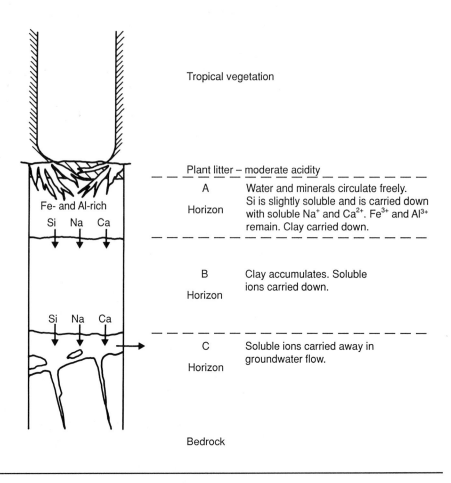

Tropical vegetation

Plant litter – moderate acidity

Fe- and Al-rich

Si   Na   Ca

A
Horizon

Water and minerals circulate freely. Si is slightly soluble and is carried down with soluble Na^+ and Ca^{2+}. Fe^{3+} and Al^{3+} remain. Clay carried down.

B
Horizon

Clay accumulates. Soluble ions carried down.

Si   Na   Ca

C
Horizon

Soluble ions carried away in groundwater flow.

Bedrock

Figure 2.13
The formation of calcic soils.
In some arid parts of the world irrigation with fresh water has eventually caused the soil to become saline (salt). How does this occur?

Sparse grassland

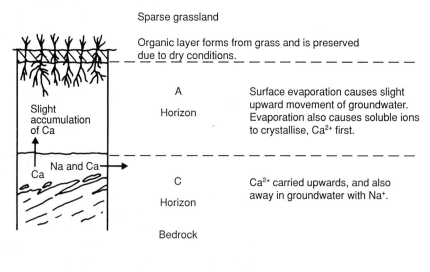

Organic layer forms from grass and is preserved due to dry conditions.

Slight accumulation of Ca

A
Horizon

Surface evaporation causes slight upward movement of groundwater. Evaporation also causes soluble ions to crystallise, Ca^{2+} first.

Na and Ca

Ca

C
Horizon

Ca^{2+} carried upwards, and also away in groundwater with Na^+.

Bedrock

rainfall, the evaporation of surface water causes groundwater to rise in the soil. Any dissolved ions transported up from the bedrock and the C horizon are deposited at the base of the A horizon by the evaporation. Thus a layer rich in calcium carbonate is formed. If this eventually forms a hard crust within the soil it is called **calcrete**. Since there is no net downward movement of water, no B horizon forms. Calcic soils can also form if the carbonate is transported into the area, by wind for example.

Calcretes and ancient calcic soils have been recognised in the Devonian Old Red Sandstone of South Wales. They occur as horizons within the flood plain silts deposited by meandering streams. They are good evidence that the flood plains dried out enough for vegetation to develop and soils to form between floods. Since soils take long periods of time to develop, there must have been long intervals between flood episodes of silt deposition.

In arid regions where upward water migration occurs, deposition of silica in horizons beneath the surface can form solid **silcrete** layers. **Saline soils** can also form where the evaporation causes deposition of evaporite minerals, particularly halite (NaCl).

Processes of Erosion

Erosion is the process of sediment removal. The sediment may have been decayed and loosened by weathering or may be removed directly from the parent rock by erosion. An essential part of the erosion process is that material is transported away from its area of origin; thus erosion and transportation are very closely linked. The main agents of erosion are: gravity; moving water; wind; ice.

Erosion by Gravity

Materials that have been loosened by weathering and then fall or slide away from the parent rock are being eroded primarily by gravity (often assisted by fluids, see the Processes of Transportation section on page 23). Falling fragments may collide with other loose fragments causing these to be carried down under the influence of gravity as well.

Erosion by Fluids

Water and air are both fluids, so their movement causes erosion in a similar way. The force of wind alone can cause erosion of bare rock surfaces only when fragments have been greatly weakened and loosened by weathering. Thus wind erosion is not a major process on bare rock but it is important on soils that are poorly bound by vegetation in arid regions. Erosion of exhausted soil was the main cause of the 'dust bowl' conditions of the American West in the 1930s. Appreciable amounts of soil are also lost from the fenland region of eastern England every year after ploughing and before the new crop growth in the spring.

Desert areas lose vast quantities of silt by wind erosion every year and the effect of this is to gradually lower the desert surface. This **deflation** causes coarser material to become concentrated on the surface, forming loose rock desert areas known by the Arabic term of *reg* (pronounced like 'leg'). Wind force can have a more destructive effect from time to time as those who have lost roofing tiles in storms or who have survived hurricanes will know.

If a flat-lying bed of loose sediment is subjected to a rainstorm, a sequence of erosional features is produced by the water. First, individual raindrops cause **rain pits** in the surface. The impact of each drop forms a small crater with the material from the crater forming a raised lip around the rim. Soon the sediment becomes saturated with water so that water can no longer infiltrate down into the sediment but must flow over the surface as surface runoff. This begins as a thin sheet of water flowing downslope, called **sheet wash**. However, if you have studied water flowing down a window pane in a rainstorm you will know that flowing sheets of water are unstable and soon break up into twisting rivulets. The small rivulets that form on the unconsolidated sediment surface are called **rills**. These soon erode small, flat-based channels called **rill marks**, which can frequently be seen on sandy beaches. As the rainstorm continues, the rills join together downslope, forming larger currents which erode still deeper channels called **gullies**. Gullies usually have fairly steep sides and are 'V' shaped in cross-section. Water from the gullies passes into streams and eventually into rivers and the sea, eroding and transporting sediment all the way.

Since rain pits and rills can only form on sediment which is above water level, they are good indicators of sediment that was deposited by water but dried out after the water drained away. Unfortunately, they are frequently eroded during the next sedimentary event and so are rarely preserved.

Running water erodes unconsolidated sediment and also bare rock in various ways. Erosion by pressure of water alone is called **hydraulic action**. Hydraulic action is most important where water is continually pounding against rock surfaces as in waterfalls and wave-beaten sea cliffs. Associated with hydraulic action is the process of **cavitation**, where water hitting the rock traps small pockets of air in cavities. The air expands explosively as the water retreats, weakening and eventually eroding the rock. Storm waves and floods can cause enormous damage to man-made and natural structures by hydraulic action.

Both wind and water are much more effective agents of erosion when they are armed with rock fragments or sand. The grinding effect of the sediment against rock is called **abrasion**. In this process, the sediment particles become ground down and this is called **attrition**. Abrasion removes sediment, attrition grinds it down into progressively smaller particles.

Wind abrasion or sand blasting is very obvious in rocky desert regions (called by the Arabic *hamada*), and forms upstanding rocky structures with strange shapes, as shown in Figure 2.14.

Figure 2.14
The sculpturing of bedrock by desert wind.
Why does the greatest erosion occur near the base of the pinnacle?

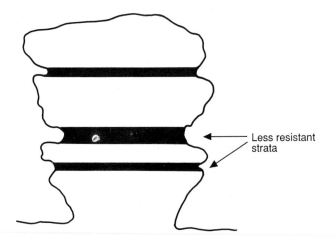

Less resistant strata

Water abrasion is very effective in rocky coastal areas causing cliff undercutting and collapse. Progressive undercutting and collapse causes cliff retreat, creating broad **wave-cut platforms** such as the one cut across the west Pembrokeshire coast in Wales, which has now become raised to a height of about 40 metres. The sediment produced by the collapsing cliff undergoes attrition to become the shingle and sand of beaches and some of the mud of tidal flats.

In upland rivers abrasion of the rock river bed causes downcutting and valley formation; most of the sand carried by these rivers is produced by attrition. In lowland rivers the processes of meandering involve the abrasion of outer banks of meanders, causing undercutting and collapse.

Erosion by Ice

Modern glaciers in temperate regions are not frozen to the ground but slide over the bedrock surface. This surface is lubricated by water produced by the pressure melting of ice. If the water at the base freezes, in winter for example, it can freeze around projecting pieces of bedrock. Ice movement then causes the bedrock to be wrenched off, a process known as **plucking**.

In valley glaciers where erosion of the valley floor has removed the rock and replaced it by lower density ice, the pressure on the underlying rock is not as great. This stress release causes the rock to fracture and move upwards, producing loose blocks which are then carried away by the ice.

A much more important ice erosion process than plucking is the abrasion caused by rock fragments being dragged along the bedrock at the base of the glacier. This produces scratches or **striations** on both the bedrock and the rock particles. The abrasion of the rock and attrition of the particles produce large quantities of very fine-grained rock flour which is eventually released by the glacier on melting. It is this fine sediment, deposited by melting ice, which is the 'clay' of 'boulder clay' (or **till**). It also forms the **varves** (finely laminated sediment) of glacial lakes and the widespread wind-blown **loess** deposits of silt grade associated with some ice sheets. Rivers draining glacial areas are a milky green colour due to the fine-grained rock flour being carried in suspension.

Polar glaciers are frozen to the bedrock for most – if not all – of the time and so their overall erosive effect is much less than that of temperate glaciers.

Structural Controls on Erosion

Natural landscapes are not flat for two reasons. Firstly, different rock types weather and erode at different rates, forming higher and lower land areas. Secondly, the structures within the rocks produce great variability. The effect that the weaknesses produced by these structures has on weathering was discussed on page 15.

In regions where some of the sedimentary rocks are resistant to erosion (e.g. sandstone, limestone) and others are not (e.g. clay, shale), the dip of the rocks is an important control on the landforms produced, as shown in Figure 2.15. Folded rocks frequently have joints concentrated near the crests of anticlines and accelerated erosion of the well-jointed crests can produce **'inverted topography'** as shown in Figure 2.16. Synclines then form the hills or mountains (such as Snowdon) and anticlines the valleys.

In granites and massive sandstones, weathering and erosion are faster where joints are closely spaced and tors are produced in the areas where the joints are widely separated (see Figure 2.17).

Where faulting has brought rocks with low resistance to erosion against rocks with high resistance to erosion, faults produce **fault scarps**, upfaulted blocks produce **horsts** or **block mountains** and downfaulted blocks produce **grabens** or **rift valleys** (see Figure 2.18).

Thus the processes of weathering and erosion acting together cause **denudation** (wearing away) at different rates and so produce the enormous variety of landscape and scenery found on Earth.

Processes of Transportation

Transportation is the movement of eroded sediment away from its source to the area where it will eventually become deposited. All sediment transport acts under the influence of gravity which causes the transportation agents of water and ice to move

Figure 2.15
Landforms formed on strata of different dips with varying resistance to erosion.
(Note: landforms similar to these can be produced in other ways.) What inland landforms would a broad open anticline in sandstones and clays produce? (Examine the Wealden anticline in Kent.) How might vertical strata produce stacks? (Examine the Needles rocks off the western end of the Isle of Wight.)

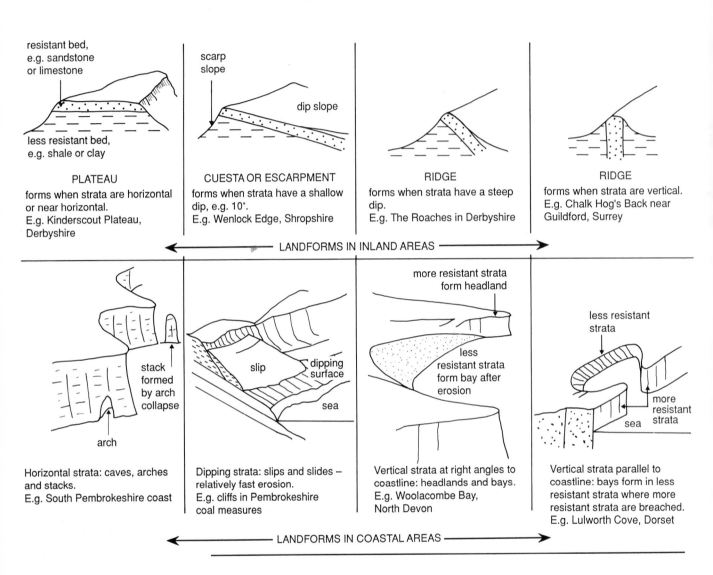

downslope and causes wind-blown sand accumulations to form mostly in lowland areas. The overall effect of transportation is to carry sediment to the lowest areas of the Earth's surface where it has the least potential energy and so is most stable.

Transportation processes can be grouped into those that are active in fluids (water and air), those that involve ice, and a large and varied group of processes known as mass gravity transport.

Processes of Mass Gravity Transport

Mass gravity transport takes place on land (where it is known as **mass movement** or **mass wasting**) and under water. It can involve large or small volumes of material, it can be very slow or catastrophically fast and it can involve large or small volumes of lubricating fluid (usually water, sometimes air). In view of this variety, these processes have been classified in a number of different ways. Geologists are mainly concerned with the different types of sediment produced by the processes. The classification used in Figure 2.19 reflects this, for it is based on the sediment products and how they have been altered during transport.

Figure 2.16
The formation of 'inverted topography'.
Why are the strata of the synclinal troughs especially resistant to erosion?

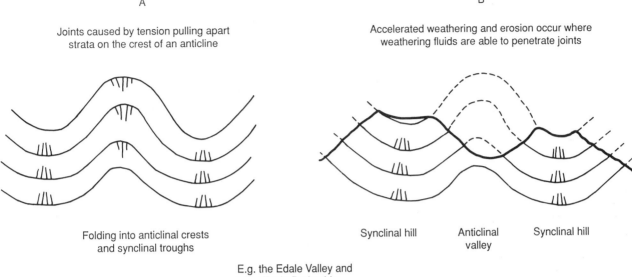

A

Joints caused by tension pulling apart
strata on the crest of an anticline

B

Accelerated weathering and erosion occur where
weathering fluids are able to penetrate joints

Folding into anticlinal crests
and synclinal troughs

Synclinal hill   Anticlinal   Synclinal hill
                   valley

E.g. the Edale Valley and
Mam Tor in Derbyshire

Vertical cross-sections

Figure 2.17
The formation of tors.
Tors form in massive, jointed rocks such as granites and coarse sandstones. What is the
importance of the water table in tor formation?

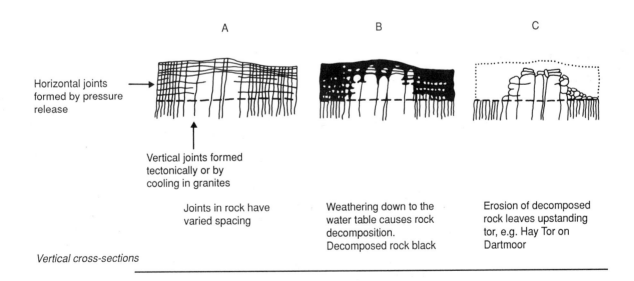

A   B   C

Horizontal joints
formed by pressure
release

Vertical joints formed
tectonically or by
cooling in granites

Joints in rock have
varied spacing

Weathering down to the
water table causes rock
decomposition.
Decomposed rock black

Erosion of decomposed
rock leaves upstanding
tor, e.g. Hay Tor on
Dartmoor

Vertical cross-sections

This classification shows that at one end of the spectrum solid material behaves in a
brittle way, breaking away from the parent rock and moving downslope without
becoming deformed. However, as factors like the amount of fluid contained become
more important, the material becomes less and less **competent** (i.e. has less and less
internal strength) and so deforms plastically by bending and flowing, eventually
becoming like a liquid in normal fluid flow. The sediments produced by these
processes show a range of structures from no deformation through to slight bending,
folding and wildly contorted folding, to complete loss of any original bedding or
structure.

Figure 2.18
Landforms produced by faulting.
Why do faults that reach the surface only produce major landforms when the strata involved have differing resistance to erosion?

A

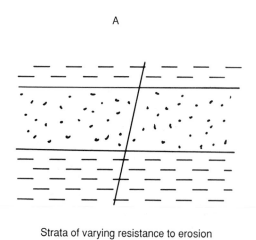

Strata of varying resistance to erosion

B

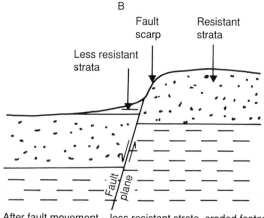

After fault movement – less resistant strata eroded fastest leaving fault scarp, e.g. Craven Fault scarp near Ingleton, western Yorkshire Dales

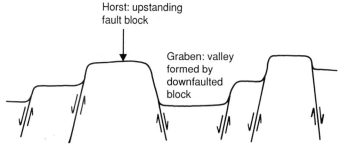

Formation of horsts and grabens in rocks of differing resistance to erosion

Rockfall (Figure 2.19, A)

Rockfall occurs when material on a steep face is loosened by weathering or erosion and falls down the face to accumulate as a sloping pile of debris called **talus** or **scree** at the bottom. The fall can involve small pieces of rock or large fragments that break up during the fall. **Scree slopes** and **talus cones** are common in upland areas of Britain, one of the best known examples being the screes on the margin of Wastwater in the Lake District which are 400 metres long. Scree running, in which the runner avalanches down the scree with the material which he has loosened, is a popular, if rather dangerous, way of descending loose scree. However, it is a good way to see scree processes in action! Underwater talus slopes form beneath wave-beaten cliffs and coral reefs. Angles of repose of up to 40^0 have been recorded on land, rather less under water.

Rockslide (Figure 2.19, B)

Rockslides most commonly occur where bedding dips gently away from a rock face and incompetent material like clay is overlain by massive competent material such as limestone. Large blocks can slide over the lubricating clay slope, deforming the clay but causing little deformation to the limestone.

Figure 2.19
A mass gravity transport classification.
The classification is based upon the amount of internal deformation suffered by the material during transport. Mass gravity transport processes can be classified in a number of ways. Which other classification methods might be useful?

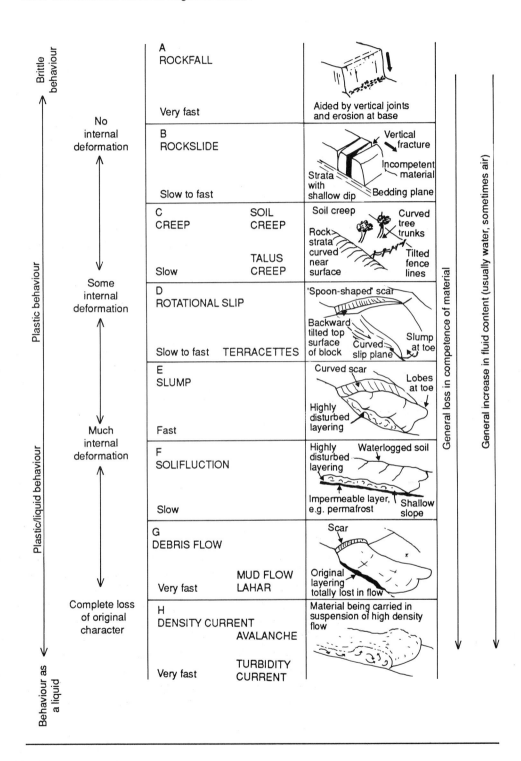

Creep (Figure 2.19, C)

Creep is a slow process that occurs on slopes of poorly consolidated material, usually by repeated expansion and contraction. The most commonly seen type of creep is **soil creep**, which causes tilted fences and walls, trees with curved lower trunks, etc. Where creep is fast, the speed of creep can be measured by placing stakes in the creeping soil, mapping their positions accurately by surveying and then carrying out a second survey months or years later. The slow creep of talus is called **talus creep**.

Rotational slip (Figure 2.19, D)

Rotational slips can form on various scales, and occur when material on a slope fails along arc-shaped planes. As it slides downhill, some small internal deformation may occur, particularly at the toe of the slip, which may become a slump deposit. Large-scale rotational slips can move fast, leaving spoon-shaped scars in cliff faces. One of the major roads across the Peak District from Manchester to Sheffield has had to be closed where a series of rotational slips occurred on a section of the road that crosses ancient slump material on the flanks of Mam Tor. Parts of the road have been carried several metres downslope and the road is unlikely to be re-opened.

The 'sheep tracks' seen on many hillsides as a series of small terraces are examples of the rotational slip process occurring on a small scale. Slip along curved planes causes the upper surfaces to become near-horizontal. While these terraces are often used by sheep, they are not formed by them; they are correctly called **terracettes**.

Slump (Figure 2.19, E)

Slumps form in poorly consolidated material which is well lubricated with water. They usually form tongues or lobes of material downslope below a spoon-shaped scar. These slump lobes can sometimes be recognised by the dome-shaped grass tussocks that grow on them. The internal structure of slump deposits is of plastic folds of various sizes trending in a variety of directions roughly downslope. A cross-section of a submarine slump on the continental slope of North Island, New Zealand, is shown in Figure 2.20. Convoluted slump deposits are frequently recognised in some ancient sediments, forming both in subaqueous deposits of various types and in aeolian sand dunes.

Figure 2.20

A submarine slump in diagrammatic cross-section.

The slump formed on the gently dipping continental slope off North Island, New Zealand (from Lewis, 1971; in Reading, 1978). How might the slump have been triggered?

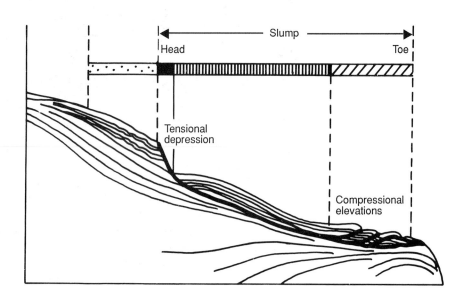

Solifluction (Figure 2.19, F)

Solifluction occurs when unconsolidated sediment becomes completely waterlogged because water cannot drain into the bedrock below. This frequently happens during the spring in permafrost areas, where the frozen subsoil prevents meltwater drainage. However, it can also occur on impermeable clay or bedrock layers on land or under water. The flow is slow but can occur on very shallow slopes and the material can become highly disturbed. Solifluction deposits or 'head' were formed in the periglaciated regions of southern England during the Pleistocene glaciations.

Debris flow (Figure 2.19, G)

Debris flows occur when unconsolidated material flows downslope very fast, often catastrophically. Debris flows can be mixtures of poorly sorted debris or they can be largely of sand, in which case they are called **sand flows,** or of mud, called **mud flows,** or of volcanic mud, called **lahars.** Large lobes of material can move downslope and over the flat land below at high speed and, on occasion, large numbers of people have been killed. An example is the Aberfan disaster of 1966 in South Wales where an old coal tip, lubricated by water, flowed downhill, engulfing part of the village and its school, killing 116 children and 28 adults. Mud flows are common on the cliffs of till in eastern England. The sight of a tongue of mud, which a few minutes before had flowed down a cliff and across a north Norfolk beach, now lying, gently steaming, on a cold winter's morning, is not easily forgotten.

Lahars are commonly associated with volcanic ash eruptions, not only because large quantities of ash are available on steep slopes but also because large supplies of water can be available. The water comes from a crater lake, from melting snow or ice or from rain produced by the thunderstorms that are frequently generated by eruptions. Lahars move fast (up to 100 km per hour) and far. In 1985 approximately 20,000 people were engulfed and died in a lahar in the Colombian town of Armero.

Density current (Figure 2.19, H)

Density currents are currents of high density fluid that flow beneath fluids of a lower density. **Avalanches** are examples of density currents on land. During the movement the snow and ice become buoyed up on air so much that they can flow down one mountainside and up the other before bouncing backwards and forwards down the valley at speeds of up to 150 km per hour. The process involves air, increased in density due to the particles of snow and ice being carried in it, flowing at the base of the normal column of air.

Underwater density currents can occur wherever fluids of two different densities meet. However, from the point of view of the geologist, the most important type is the **turbidity current.** Turbidity currents involve turbid muddy dense water flowing downslope at high speed beneath the clear water column above. They are now known to be the cause of the thick sequences of sheet-like graded rocks (called **turbidites**) that are found in many countries and were previously unexplained.

Probably the largest turbidity current of modern times was triggered by the Grand Banks earthquake of 1929, although it was not recognised as a turbidity current at the time. A thick sequence of sediment had been deposited on the edge of the Grand Banks, off Newfoundland, Canada, by the St Lawrence river. A series of submarine telegraph cables had been laid along the continental slope, continental rise and abyssal plain beneath. After the earthquake, the cables were broken in sequence down the slope to the abyssal plain and the times at which these breaks occurred were known exactly. The breaks were caused by a mass which was shown by calculation to have moved at up to 100 km per hour and travelled at least 700 kilometres (see Figure 2.21). The turbidity current was triggered when a slide or slump near the epicentre of the earthquake flowed downslope as a density current and eventually formed a sheet-like turbidite deposit over an estimated 100,000 kilometres of ocean floor. This is a fine example of how new scientific ideas can be used to understand previously unexplained events in the past.

Figure 2.21
The Grand Banks Turbidite of 1929 (after Heezen and Hollister, 1971; in Reading, 1978).
How was the velocity of the turbidity current calculated? What causes the velocity to change as it travels along?

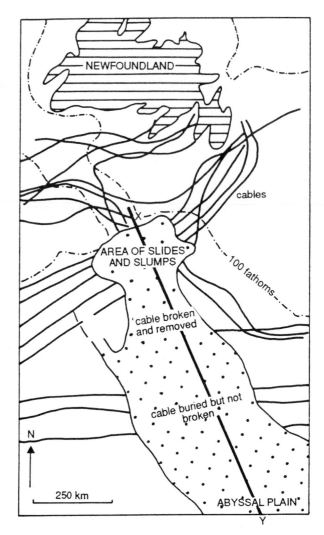

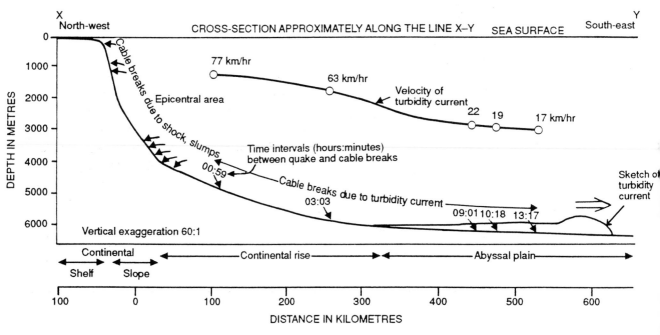

Turbidity currents and turbidites have now been recognised in many other parts of the world. Much of the sediment deposited on ocean floors and in submarine trenches has now been shown by seismic evidence to be of turbidity current origin.

Another type of density current important to geological studies is the ***nuée ardente*** or glowing cloud. These white-hot ash clouds flow downhill in some violent volcanic eruptions, such as that of Mt. Pelee on the Caribbean island of Martinique in 1902. This travelled at up to 100 kilometres per hour and wiped out the 30,000 population of the town of St Pierre.

Many of the mass movements described are first triggered by earthquakes or sometimes by man-made shocks. The mass gravity transport movements frequently grade into one another so that a rotational slip may become a slump, eventually producing a debris flow and density current as more and more water or air is taken into the movement. **Landslide** is the general term used to describe all large-scale mass movements on land.

Fluid Transportation Processes

Transportation by moving fluids

The processes of sediment erosion, transportation and deposition can be studied experimentally in the lab by using a **flume**. Most lab flumes are long glass boxes, open at the top, through which water can flow at different rates. These artificial channels allow the scientist to measure water discharge (the volume of water passing through the channel in a given time), velocity and depth, and to observe and measure sediment movement and the formation of sedimentary structures (see Figure 2.22). In this way the links between water velocity and sediment movement can be understood.

Figure 2.22
A flume, an artificial channel constructed in the laboratory for experimentation purposes.
Water depth, velocity and discharge and sediment grade and quantity can be varied. How might the discharge in m³ per sec. be calculated?

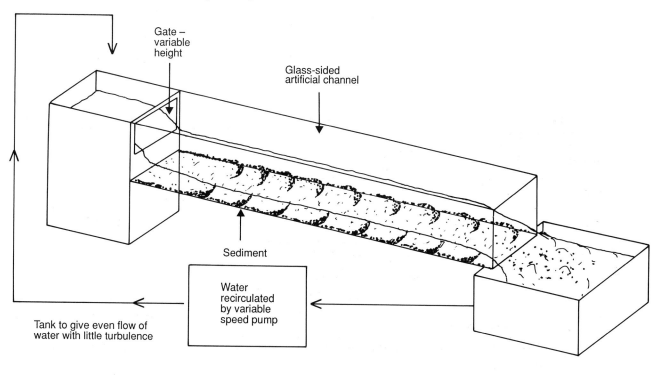

Making and Moving Sediment

When sediment is first picked up from the bed of a channel (eroded) it is said to be **entrained**. Sediments of different sizes are entrained at different current velocities. This has been studied experimentally by placing sand of known grain size in the flume bed and steadily increasing the flow velocity until the grains first begin to move. The water velocity at this point is the **critical erosion velocity** or **entrainment velocity**. If similar experiments are carried out for sediments of different sizes, then a graph can be plotted showing grain size against entrainment velocity, as in Figure 2.23. This shows that for material coarser than sand grade, the coarser the material, the higher the velocity of current necessary for erosion. However, for loose or unconsolidated material finer than sand grade there is no link between sediment size and the velocity needed for erosion. The graph also shows that silts and clays that have had time to harden and consolidate (and so become cohesive) need higher current velocities for erosion. Thus sands are more easily eroded than consolidated muds. This property of fine sediment to resist erosion has been used by canal engineers who line canals with clay. The clay minerals swell when wet and so make the canal waterproof. This works well for the low velocity currents found in canals because the swollen clay coheres (sticks) and resists erosion. But when there is a leak, high velocity water flows through the leak causing great erosion and catastrophic failure of the canal bank. Not only are canal boats then left high and dry but fields are flooded and people may be killed.

Finally, the graph in Figure 2.23 shows that once sediment has been eroded, it can be transported by currents of lower velocity than those needed for erosion. At even lower velocities, the sediment can no longer be transported and deposition takes place.

The theoretical current force necessary to move unconsolidated grains of known size and density on beds of given slope and roughness can be calculated mathematically. If the results of these calculations for different sediment sizes are plotted on a graph then the plots obtained are very similar to those obtained by the experimental flume work. By approaching the same problem in these two ways we can check the results and gain a deeper understanding of the whole process.

Experiments and calculations on wind erosion show that the processes involved are the same as those in water erosion. Due to the differences in density and the viscosity of the fluid (air), however, sediment of smaller grain size is involved.

Figure 2.23
Plot of grain size against entrainment velocity.
The experiments were first carried out and the graph plotted by Hjulstrom (later modified and published in this form by Sundborg, 1956; in Collinson and Thompson, 1982). The plot shows the current velocities necessary to erode and transport sediments of various grades. How does the drying out of mud affect the velocity of current necessary for its erosion?

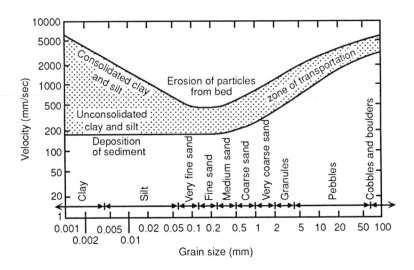

During erosion, some of the sediment may have become dissolved and is then carried by the water as **dissolved load**. The particles of sediment are transported either as **suspended load** or **bedload**. Bedload transport can easily be observed on a stream table in a lab or wherever clear water flows over sand, such as in a stream or on a beach. Some of the grains can be seen to jump downstream in a series of jumps of roughly equal length. Other grains, particularly the larger ones, can be seen to roll while others, generally the flatter ones, slide downstream. The jumping motion is called **saltation**, as shown in Figure 2.24. After hitting the bed the grains rise high into the current and then fall back to the bed as they move downstream. The processes of rolling and sliding, where grains are always in contact with the bed, are together called **traction**.

In muddy waters, the mud is fine-grained material carried in suspension. Most natural water flows are turbulent and the eddying turbulent flow is able to buoy up small particles, against the pull of gravity, so that they are carried along without ever touching bottom. Only when the current slows and the turbulence becomes less or ceases altogether can this finer material settle out of suspension onto the bed. The settling of fine clays can be greatly assisted by the **flocculation** process caused when fresh water containing suspended clays flows into salt water. Under these conditions of changing salinity, the clay minerals flocculate together to form larger particles which then fall out of suspension at a faster rate. Clays which might otherwise stay in suspension are deposited in this way.

The Mississippi river gives a guide to the relative proportions of material carried by river water in different ways. It has been calculated that in one year 200 million tonnes of material is carried in solution, 500 million tonnes in suspension and 50 million tonnes as bedload. The easily forgotten dissolved load is thus shown to be very important.

The fairly simple picture of sediment transport shown in Figure 2.24 is more complex in practice because there are transitions between the various modes of transport. For example, some grains travel partly by saltation and partly by suspension, with the 'bounce' having a long and variable path.

Figure 2.24
The transportation of sediment.
Sediment grains can be transported in fluids (water or wind) by processes of traction, saltation (bouncing) or suspension. Water also carries dissolved ions in solution. What are the major factors that cause some grains to be carried by traction, some by saltation and some in suspension? How can the same grain be carried at times by traction, at times by saltation and at times by suspension?

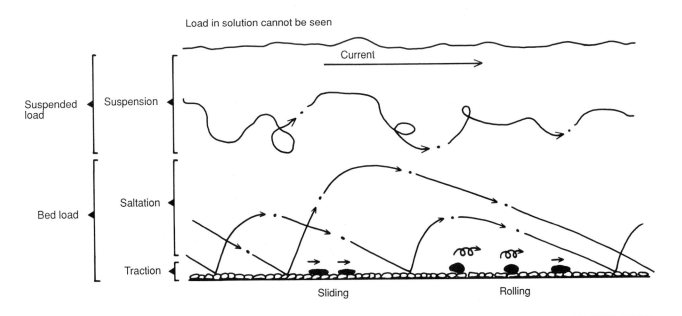

Sedimentation by slowing fluids and in still fluids

As currents slow they progressively lose their sediment-carrying capacity and the sediment is deposited. Thus in areas where there are frequent velocity changes the sediment may be eroded and deposited many times. The main depositional areas are places where the water is relatively still, such as puddles, ponds, lakes or the deep sea. In such areas fine material that has been introduced by turbulent currents, such as streams, rivers or tidal flows, settles from suspension as a continuous rain onto the floor below.

When a single current, such as a turbidity current, is slowed by entering relatively still water a single depositional event takes place. Since the coarser material falls to the bed faster than the fine material, a **graded bed** is often produced, coarse at the base and fining upwards. Similar graded beds are produced when any mass of mixed sediment is suddenly introduced to relatively still water, for example by a volcanic eruption or a melting iceberg. Thus well-formed graded beds normally indicate deposition by slowing currents or in still or fairly still water.

Fine-grained material also settles from suspension in the air, raining sediment onto the land or sea surface and this includes the ash of volcanic eruptions. However, air fall deposits of volcanic material do not form good graded beds.

Ice Transportation Processes

Material which has been eroded from the bedrock at the base of ice sheets and from the walls and floors of valley glaciers is simply carried along as dirty ice by the ice movement. There is no sorting out of coarser from finer material as there is in other forms of transportation. Valley glaciers also carry on their upper surfaces the material which falls down the valley sides. Where ice sheets and glaciers float on lakes or seas, the material is carried in the ice along the surface of the water. When the ice melts the material is deposited as till or is reworked by the meltwater streams or the sea to leave silt, sand or gravel deposits.

Economic Aspects

The Weathering of Building Stones

One of the most useful ways of investigating the effects of weathering is to study tombstones in graveyards. Very brief studies will show that some stones show much more resistance to weathering than others and that building stones are attacked by the same weathering processes that affect natural rock outcrops. An exception to this is the accelerated weathering of building stones found in cities and industrial areas.

In rural areas limestones used for building are attacked mainly by carbonation which often causes fossil fragments to stand out of the rock. In red sandstones, hydration of the iron cement may cause the released quartz grains to be quickly eroded. Freeze-thaw weathering particularly attacks fissile stones like slates and, in winter, can cause **spalling** of brick surfaces (i.e. the flaking away of surface layers). On occasion, brick and stone walls can be cracked and toppled by freeze-thaw effects, as some will know to their cost!

The accelerated weathering in city and industrial areas is caused by the polluted atmosphere which was particularly bad before the Clean Air Acts came into force. Sulphur dioxide in the atmosphere reacts with the calcium carbonate present in the stone, causing gypsum to grow in the pore spaces, which eventually causes the surfaces of the building stones to crumble away. Soot deposits react with the iron minerals in the stone, producing black surface coatings which can scale off, frequently leaving powdery, easily-eroded sediment beneath. Carbonation is accelerated in the acid atmosphere.

Some weathering problems can be rectified fairly cheaply, for example by smoothing a thin cement skin over rotting brickwork or by 'pebble dashing' walls with cement and pebbles. The mortar of brick buildings can be replaced by 'pointing' at regular intervals. It is much more expensive to replace decayed building stones in cathedrals and other similar buildings. The weathered surfaces of historical buildings and monuments can be cleaned by sand blasting, in which the natural abrasion processes of deserts are created artificially, revealing the true colour of the building stones. This too is an expensive business and the overall cost to nations of weathering must be very high indeed.

Bauxite Formation

The aluminium ore bauxite ($Al_2O_3.2H_2O$) is produced by the extensive chemical weathering of clay-rich soils under tropical or sub-tropical conditions. Under these harsh conditions the clay minerals, such as kaolinite, form bauxite by hydrolysis.

$$Al_2O_3.2SiO_2.2H_2O \;+\; 4H_2O \;\rightarrow\; Al_2O_3.2H_2O \;+\; 2H_4SiO_4$$

kaolin			bauxite	silicic acid
				carried away
				in solution

Natural bauxite, when fairly pure, is whitish but it is usually coloured by iron impurities to yellow-brown and reddish tints. It is usually found as extensive horizontal or gently tilted sheets. The major source area of bauxite for aluminium ore is the Caribbean area, particularly Jamaica.

Cliff Retreat

Fast cliff retreat is a serious problem wherever cliffs are formed of poorly consolidated materials which have been built over by man. It is a particular problem in the Pleistocene till cliffs of East Anglia and much of the east coast of England, and in the Mesozoic and Tertiary clay cliffs of southern England. The sea undercuts the cliffs by wave action at beach level causing the unsupported cliff to fail in rotational slips, slumps and other types of landslide. Houses and roads built on the cliff top can be carried away and destroyed in such mass movements. Maintenance of some parts of the coastal paths can also be difficult due to this problem.

Heavy Mineral Accumulations

The transportation of sediment by fluids depends not only upon the size of the sediment but also on its density. The density of minerals is given as the relative density (R.D.); this is the ratio of the density of the mineral to water which has a density of 1 gm cm^{-3}. Since relative density is a ratio, it has no units.

Dense minerals are heavier and so are more difficult to erode than less dense minerals of the same size, like quartz sand (R.D. 2.65). Dense minerals are also deposited more quickly, thus water currents provide natural concentration processes for heavy minerals. Alluvial gold, as found in Australia, Alaska, South Africa and, to a lesser extent, in many other parts of the world, including the southern uplands of Scotland, is formed in this way. The dense gold particles (R.D. 15 – 20) are found near the base of stream and river deposits and are associated with the coarse-grained sediment. In 'panning', water is made to flow round and round a pan which contains a little gold-bearing sediment. The gold concentrates beneath the sediment at the base of the pan. Another example of the natural concentration processes of water being used to recover gold is where crushed gold ore is flushed down a chute by water and the gold builds up behind baffles, or low barriers, that are built across the chute.

Heavy mineral accumulations are called **placer** deposits. Other important placer deposits are the rubies and sapphires (R.D. about 4) of Burma, the diamonds (R.D. 3.5) of West Africa and the tin deposits (R.D. of cassiterite about 7) of South East Asia. Alluvial tin is also worked in Cornwall where erosion of the tin mine spoil heaps has carried the unrecovered tin into local streams and concentrated it there.

Waves concentrate heavy minerals by the same processes as water currents and continuously pounding waves provide an enormous source of energy for concentration purposes. Some important beach placers are the diamond deposits of Namibia, the gold deposits of Nome in Alaska and the deposits of the titanium ore ilmenite (R.D. about 5) in India. Beach tin can also be found in Cornwall.

Some of the bands of dark minerals seen on beaches are heavy mineral deposits concentrated by wave action. However, these should not be confused with bands of dark-coloured low-density materials like charcoal which can also be concentrated into bands by waves.

Practical Investigation and Fieldwork

The best way to understand the processes active in the formation of sediment is by experimentation and fieldwork. Much of the information described in this chapter has been gained by these means. You too will gain a much better understanding of these processes by carrying out experiments, such as some of the ones suggested below. In this way you will be conducting your own scientific investigations. Record your observations and results in a methodical and scientific manner.

1. How does freeze-thaw weathering affect different types of rocks?
Take two specimens each of limestone, sandstone, shale, granite, etc. Soak one specimen of each rock type in water overnight. Wrap all the specimens in plastic 'cling-film'. Place all the specimens in the freezing compartment of a refrigerator or deepfreeze until frozen, then remove them and allow them to thaw. Repeat this as often as possible for a week. Then carefully unwrap the specimens and examine them. What effect does the water have on the freezing and thawing of each rock? Which rock types are most susceptible to freeze-thaw weathering?

2. Does water expand on freezing? If so, by how much?
Take a plastic syringe (as found in most labs and hospitals) and seal the needle end by melting in a bunsen flame. Fill the syringe with 20 ml of water and place a thin piece of wire down inside the syringe. Push the plunger down to the water surface (the wire will allow the air to escape) and remove the wire. Freeze as in the investigation above. Measure the amount of expansion, if any. The percentage expansion of water on freezing is calculated by dividing the amount of expansion by the original volume of water (20 ml) and multiplying by 100. (This experiment was first described by Williams, 1984).

3. How do the colours of oxidised and reduced iron compounds compare?
In the lab, react small quantities of iron (III) chloride ($FeCl_3$) with sodium hydroxide to produce iron (III) hydroxide.

$$FeCl_3 + 3NaOH \rightarrow Fe(OH)_3 + 3NaCl$$

Observe the colour of the dissolved Fe ions in solution: this is oxidised iron. Repeat the experiment with iron (III) sulphate ($FeSO_4$) and sodium hydroxide.

$$FeSO_4 + 2NaOH \rightarrow Fe(OH)_2 + Na_2SO_4$$

Observe the colour of the dissolved Fe ions in solution: this is reduced iron. Add an oxidising agent such as hydrogen peroxide to the solution of reduced iron and explain the results.

4. What is the angle of repose of loose sediment?
When loose sediment falls onto the Earth's surface, on a scree slope for example, it forms sloping beds of material. The angle of the slope is called the **angle of repose** (or **angle of rest**). This can be measured for various types of sediment, from fine sand to scree, using a clinometer or a protractor on a horizontal surface. Place two wooden blocks together and pour some of the sediment onto the junction between the two blocks. Then carefully move one of the blocks away. The sediment will pour into the gap, adopting its angle of repose which should be measured as an angle from the horizontal. The results should be plotted on a graph of angle of repose against grain

size. The experiment can be repeated underwater if metal blocks are used. Do sediments have a steeper or less steep angle of repose under water? The effects of sediment angularity can be investigated by comparing angular scree material with rounded river gravel of the same size. **Angles of yield** can be measured by gently tilting one of the blocks until the sediment becomes unstable and the slope collapses. The angle measured just before the collapse is the angle of yield. How does the angle of yield compare with the angle of repose?

5. How does sediment change during transport?
Many tropical beaches are composed entirely of carbonate sand. This experiment investigates how this sand can form and change during wave transport. Collect assorted whole sea shells and other remnants of beach life (e.g. seaweed, dead crabs, etc.). In the lab sort the remnants into groups of organisms of the same type and weigh each group. Measure the largest individuals of each group. Record all the results. Place the material into a polythene bottle with some beach pebbles of a similar size and shake vigorously for one minute. Then sort the material into groups again, placing the unrecognisable material and pebbles back into the bottle. Weigh and measure the groups again, recording the results. Repeat the experiment on the same material several times. Plot the results onto two graphs, one for the weight of each group against total shaking time, the other for the size of the largest individual of each group against total shaking time. The graphs show how the sedimentary particles have been broken down during the simulated transport, and which groups have the highest survival rates and are thus most likely to be preserved. Examine the carbonate sand produced (using a hand lens) and describe its characteristics in terms of average size, range of sediment size and shape of particles. (This experiment is based on one described by Kennett, 1983.)

6. How is sediment transported by water?
Set up a metal or plastic tray so that one end overhangs a sink and the tray dips gently in the direction of the sink. Place a large beaker in the sink beneath the lower end of the tray. Place a bed of river or beach sand about 10 mm deep in the tray. Allow water to flow from a rubber tube or hose into the top end of the tray; the water will eventually overflow at the lower end into the beaker. The beaker will also overflow eventually, leaving any sediment washed from the tray in the bottom (blocked sinks are avoided in this way). This is a working stream table. Leave it for a few minutes to develop.

Examine and describe the following processes (some of these are explained later in this book – see index):

a) erosion of the channel bed and of the channel bank causing undercutting and collapse, winnowing of fine sediment, scour around obstacles;
b) transportation by rolling, sliding, saltating and in suspension;
c) sorting by particle size and particle density;
d) deposition by a waning current on flat and inclined beds.

The following erosional structures may form and should be examined: rills, channels, scours, channel lags. The following depositional structures may form: deposition as sand bars on the insides of channel bends, formation of sand shadows downstream of obstacles. Depositional structures in the standing water at the lower end of the tray can include microdelta formation such as delta top, delta front and prodelta, distributary channels, delta lobes, abandoned lobes and cross bedding. If the standing water is muddy and is left to stand overnight, clay drapes will be deposited. Experiments on the formation of rain pits may be carried out by dropping water from a teat pipette. Experiments on the relationships between channel depth and discharge, and the size of largest particle moved and discharge may also be carried out. (Note: stream tables may be bought commercially or may be made quite simply and easily. See King, 1981.)

7. How does flowing water sort sediment according to density?
Set up a stream table as described in No. 6, but with a bed of mixed fine sand and coarse-grained carborundum powder (an abrasive powder used in polishing rock). Observe how during the flow the lower density sand becomes separated from the higher density

carborundum powder. Describe the results. After the run is completed, allow the water to drain for several hours and then use a ruler to cut vertical faces through the sediment. Observe and describe the sediment sorting visible in these faces. The heavy mineral accumulations are small-scale placer deposits.

8. How does sediment settle from suspension?
This experiment needs a tall glass tube: coffee jars are good, measuring jars better and burettes even better. Fill the tube nearly to the top with water. Take sediment containing a range of sediment sizes and add some water to make it damp. If using measuring cylinders or coffee jars, add a handful, if using a burette add a small quantity using a funnel. Leave to settle. Observe the production of a graded bed, coarse at the base, fining upwards. Graded bed sequences can be produced by repeating the addition of sediment several times.

9. How long does sediment take to reach the bottom of the ocean?
Fill two burettes nearly to the top with water. To one add a small quantity of muddy sediment and – with caution – shake vigorously. Leave the two burettes standing and observe them carefully at intervals. Record how long it takes the muddy sediment to settle so that the water becomes as clear as in the other burette. Divide this time by the length of the burette and multiply by the depth below sea level of the deepest trench (the Nero Deep of the Marianas Trench: 11,055 m). Repeat the calculation for the average depth of the Pacific Ocean (4,267 m). (Note: this calculation gives only an approximate answer since ocean currents, changes in the viscosity of sea water with temperature and the effects of using a narrow tube are not taken into account.)

10. How do particles settle through water?
Fill a glass-sided tank with water. Take a series of sedimentary particles of various types and sizes up to 20 mm across (e.g. sea shells, pieces of slate, mica, sandstone, small pebbles, pen tops, sweets of various shapes, etc.). Carefully observe and record how they fall through the water and the orientation they take on landing. Which particles fall at the fastest rates?

11. How do currents orientate particles?
Use the same tank and particles as in the investigation above but siphon off most of the water. Gently tilt the tank end-to-end to build up a wave motion. Observe and describe how the particles orientate themselves with respect to the end-to-end current. Compare the orientation of bivalve shells and any cylindrical particles with those of the investigation above. How can you tell whether such particles, if preserved in rocks, were deposited by settling or by currents? (Note: the same experiment may be carried out in a fairly shallow tray of water.)

12. What rock type is best for a tombstone?
In your local graveyard, examine the rock types, dates and conditions of the tombstones. On the basis of the data collected, rank the rock types in order of resistance to weathering in your area. Which type of rock makes the longest-lasting tombstone? Which type of rock would you prefer? Does the facing direction of the tombstone matter? Does it matter if the tombstone is under trees? Repeat the fieldwork and analysis for a graveyard in a different type of area. Attempt to explain any observed differences.

13. Which building and facing stones are the most popular?
Make a short field excursion around your nearest town or city and record all the types of building stone and stone used for facing shops and other buildings that you see. Record the number of times you see each type of stone. Analyse your results to rank the building stones in order of popularity. Attempt to explain the rank order shown by your results.

14. How do loose materials become sedimented on slopes?
Sediments on active scree slopes and wind-formed sand dunes are at their angle of repose. On a visit to a scree or dune, dislodge the sediment with your foot and observe the result. Describe the shape of the sediment lobe produced. Study the sediment

carefully to find out where the coarsest material accumulates. How is the presence of water likely to affect the sedimentation process? What will happen under water? Your ideas can be tested by experiment in the lab.

Test Your Understanding

1. Compare the resistance to weathering of various rock types. This can be done using a table similar to the one given below, which has already been filled out for granite. Copy out this table and complete it for the following rock types: basalt; sandstone; shale; limestone; marble; slate. By comparing the summary columns, rank the rocks in general order of resistance to weathering.

N.B. To assist you, the characteristics of a resistant rock have been included in the table.

Rock Types	Mineral Stability	Particle Size	Cement Type	Bedding	Cleavage	Jointing	Summary
A resistant rock	High	Fine sed. Variable igneous or metamorphic	Silica best	Little or none	None	None	
Granite	High	?	N/A	N/A	N/A	Moderate resistance	Moderate to high resistance

2. Slates rich in calcium carbonate weather quickly by splitting or scaling in urban and industrial areas. Explain why this problem occurs and why low calcium carbonate content is essential in good roofing slates.

3. The lower Jurassic Lincolnshire limestone is a soft yellow limestone where it is quarried near Grantham in Lincolnshire. The limestone is processed by laying blocks out on the ground with bedding planes vertical and leaving them over the winter. In spring they can be split into thin slabs for roofing materials, locally called 'slates'. They can be thinly split only if processed in this way. What natural process is being exploited? Explain how it works.

4. Why are exposures of Cretaceous greensand, rich in the green mineral glauconite, usually yellowy-brown in colour?

5. Attempt to classify mass movements on the basis of the following criteria: particle size; speed; sediment type.

6. When opencast workings are being excavated, the first task is to remove the topsoil and store it in a tip nearby. After the workings have been completed and the pit backfilled, the soil is replaced. Why is it necessary to store and replace the soil?

7. In the mining valleys of South Wales the tips of waste material from the coal mines are frequently situated on the valley sides. Careful studies have been carried out on the rainwater drainage patterns near the tips. Why?

8. The lobe of a newly deposited mud flow was seen to be steaming gently on a cold winter morning. Why?

9. Sand blasting is the commercial process used for cleaning the building stones of historical buildings. In the process, sand is blown at the surface of the stone by compressed air at high velocity. Rank the following building stones in order of those cleaned most easily to those hardest to clean by this method: granite, basalt, sandstone, limestone, slate, marble. Explain your rankings.

10. If a sewer were partially blocked by a layer of loose sediment, how might the sediment best be removed by adapting a natural process?

11. Sands are analysed for heavy minerals by using the heavy liquid bromoform (R.D. 2.95) followed by use of the binocular microscope. How might the analysis be carried out?

12. In the Bovey Tracey area of south-eastern Devon, a thick sequence of clays occupies a shallow basin. The deposit was laid down during the Oligocene (mid-Tertiary) and the clays are composed mostly of kaolinite. In places the clay layers are interbedded with organic material and they interfinger with gravel beds at the margins of the deposit. The clays are exploited for pottery making, building bricks, tiles, etc. and are called ball clays because they were originally extracted in lump-like balls. What is the most likely history of formation of this deposit?

3. WHAT CAN THE PARTICLES TELL US?

Analysing Sediment

We have seen that sediments form in a variety of ways and that the processes involved in their formation leave their marks on individual grains, beds and sequences. By careful study of the sediments therefore, we can usually understand the processes by which they were formed. The necessary investigations range in scale from detailed studies of single particles to studying the sediment body as a whole. Individual particles can give many clues to the origin of the sediment. For example, the main processes by which chalk was formed were only understood when it became possible to examine the grains using a scanning electron microscope (chalk particles are so small they have to be measured in microns, i.e. thousandths of millimetres). This detailed examination revealed that the grains are largely calcareous microfossils called coccoliths which accumulated on the floor of a warm, quiet sea.

The particles of sediments and sedimentary rocks are described by five main properties. The two most important of these are **particle composition** (i.e. the kinds of particles and their abundance) and **particle size**. The other three properties can be very important in some circumstances, less so in others; they are **particle shape**, **particle orientation** and **packing** of the particles. The properties of particle size, shape, orientation and packing together determine the **texture** of the rock. In sedimentary rocks which are difficult to break down into individual particles, the properties can be determined by careful examination of the rock surface using a hand lens, or of thin sections under a microscope.

Particle Composition

Analysing the Composition

Sedimentary grains are composed either of crystals of single minerals or of fragments of rock or fossil. To analyse the composition of a sedimentary rock, the individual minerals must be identified and their abundance in the rock calculated. While large numbers of minerals can occur in sediments, fortunately most sediments can be described and understood by identifying only the more common minerals present.

The sediment classification systems used by geologists are mainly applied to sedimentary rocks, but they can be used for unconsolidated (loose) sediments as well. Sedimentary rocks which contain only one mineral (monomineralic rocks) are dealt with fairly easily. A rock containing only halite is called rock salt. A rock composed only of calcium carbonate (calcite or aragonite) is called limestone (although some limestones are not pure calcium carbonate). A sandstone containing only quartz sand is called a quartz arenite or orthoquartzite. When more than one mineral is involved, however, rock description and classification become more complicated. Many different classification systems have been evolved to deal with this problem.

41

What Can the Particles Tell Us?

The variation of rock composition is easiest to see if plotted on a graph. The type of graph most commonly used is the triangular diagram, which has the advantage of being able to plot the variation between three factors. An example is shown in Figure 3.1. In this example the diagram plots the variation between the three end members X, Y and Z.

Figure 3.1
Use of a triangular diagram.
This diagram plots the variation between end members X, Y and Z. What do the plots at positions S and T contain?

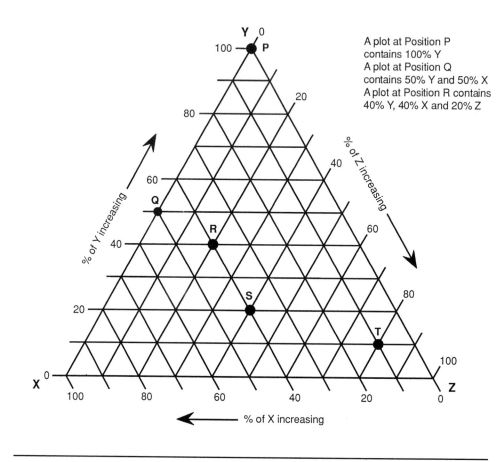

A plot at Position P contains 100% Y
A plot at Position Q contains 50% Y and 50% X
A plot at Position R contains 40% Y, 40% X and 20% Z

The sandstone (or arenite) classification system shown in Figure 3.2 is based upon three of the constituents of sandstone which are easily recognisable, namely quartz (clear and glassy to milky coloured, no cleavage), feldspar (dull surface, white or pink in colour, often with shiny cleavage surfaces) and rock (lithic) fragments (fragments of an original rock that has become eroded). Using this system, a sandstone containing more than 95 per cent quartz is called a quartz arenite; with more than 25 per cent feldspar (and less than 50 per cent rock fragments) it is an arkosic arenite, and a rock plotting at position A is a sublitharenite.

One problem with this system is that it takes no account of the mud matrix found in some sandstones, particularly those deposited by turbidity currents. Thus the system has been extended into a 'fourth dimension' to take account of this, as shown in Figure 3.3. On this rather complicated system, sandstones containing less than 15 per cent mud matrix are classified as in Figure 3.2. Sandstones with 15 per cent or more matrix are called wackes with the most common type being greywacke of either feldspathic or lithic type. Should the rock contain more than 75 per cent mud, it is called a **mudstone**. A simple way of working this system is to remember that most sandy rocks

Figure 3.2
A classification system for sandstones (after Pettijohn et al., 1973; in Tucker, 1982).
What names are given to sandstones with the following compositions:
a) 80% quartz, 15% feldspar, 5% rock fragments;
b) 97% quartz, 3% feldspar, 0% rock fragments;
c) 55% quartz, 12% feldspar, 33% rock fragments?

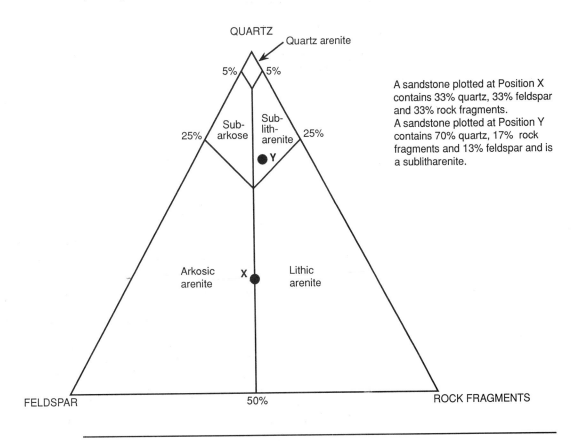

A sandstone plotted at Position X contains 33% quartz, 33% feldspar and 33% rock fragments.
A sandstone plotted at Position Y contains 70% quartz, 17% rock fragments and 13% feldspar and is a sublitharenite.

that contain more than 15 per cent matrix are **greywackes**, most that contain more than 25 per cent feldspar are **arkosic arenites** (often simply called **arkoses**), and those that contain over 95 per cent quartz are **quartz arenites** (often called **orthoquartzites**). The rest can simply be called **sandstones**.

Rocks that contain more than 50 per cent calcium carbonate are called **limestones** and are easy to recognise as they give strong reactions with dilute hydrochloric acid (HCl). There are several different types of limestone but as their classification is based upon the type and size of the grains, rather than their chemical composition, this will be dealt with in the next section. Carbonate rocks that contain a high percentage of dolomite ($CaMg(CO_3)_2$), which reacts strongly only with warm dilute hydrochloric acid, are called **dolomites**.

Ironstones are rich in iron minerals that usually weather to a rusty yellow or brown colour. They often feel more dense than other sedimentary rocks.

Cherts (and **flints**) are composed of very fine-grained (or cryptocrystalline) silica and occur as hard, usually dark-coloured, beds and nodules.

Greensands are sandstones that contain a high percentage of the green mineral glauconite (which usually oxidises on weathering to yellow-brown limonite).

Micaceous sandstones contain a high percentage of sheet-like mica particles lying along the bedding planes. The mica is usually muscovite, which is more stable than the other micas.

Figure 3.3
A classification system for sandstones containing matrix (after Pettijohn et al., 1973; in Tucker, 1982).
What names are given to sandstones with the following compositions:
a) 10% matrix, sand grains are 50% quartz, 50% feldspar;
b) 25% matrix, sand grains are 50% quartz, 50% rock fragments?

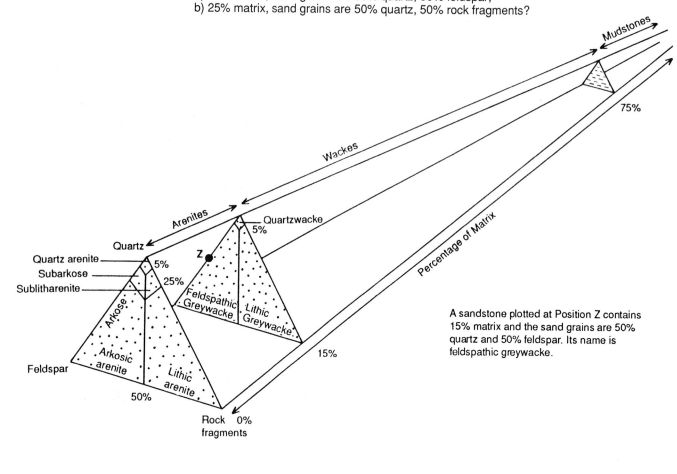

A sandstone plotted at Position Z contains 15% matrix and the sand grains are 50% quartz and 50% feldspar. Its name is feldspathic greywacke.

What Can the Composition Tell Us?

If the mineral composition is studied carefully and the principle of uniformitarianism (i.e. that the present is the key to the past) is applied, we can gain important insights into the ancient depositional environments, as the following examples show.

In sediments that have been transported a long way, either by a river or in beach or shallow sea conditions, the unstable minerals break down and the sediment becomes more mature. Therefore sandstones like arkoses which contain a high proportion of feldspar are immature and have not been transported far from their source rocks. Quartz-rich sediments like orthoquartzites are very mature and so have been transported long distances or may be **polycyclic**. The particles of polycyclic sediments have been around the sedimentary cycle (see Figure 2.1, p. 6) more than once.

The production of calcium carbonate sediments is greatest under tropical or near-tropical conditions and so the presence of large amounts of calcium carbonate in a sediment (which therefore is probably a limestone) is usually taken to indicate a warm depositional environment. Sedimentary ironstones are not forming on Earth today but those that contain ooids (small spherical particles) probably also formed in warm seas. Glauconite forms today only on the floors of shallow seas and so greensands must therefore be shallow sea sandstones. Mica flakes are not deposited in the turbulent wind-blown conditions of deserts and are rarely deposited in active river channels.

They are able to settle out of suspension only in quiet water conditions and so indicate a quiet subaqueous environment of deposition. Micaceous turbidite sandstones, deposited by slowing turbidity currents are fairly common.

Particle Size and Sorting

Particle Size Analysis

The most important part of the texture of a sediment or sedimentary rock is the particle size which, like particle composition, is a critical part of the description of most sediments and rock types. Since most sediments contain particles that have a range of sizes, it is the mean or average grain size that is used in description. The grain size of clastic rocks (i.e. non-carbonate rocks) is usually described using the Wentworth-Udden scale shown in Figure 3.4.

Figure 3.4
The Wentworth-Udden grade scale for clastic sediments.
Particle diameters in mm are correlated with the ϕ scale. Sediment and rock names are shown. What names are given to clastic rocks with the following grain sizes: 6ϕ; 1.5ϕ; 3ϕ; 77mm; 0.1mm?

ϕ values	*Particle diameter (mm diam.)*	*Wentworth grades*	*Rock name*
		Boulders	Conglomerate
-8	256		
		Cobbles	Conglomerate
-6	64		
		Pebbles	Conglomerate
-2	4		
		Granules	Granulestone
-1	2		
		Very coarse sand	Sandstone
0	1		
		Coarse sand	Sandstone
1	0.5		
		Medium sand	Sandstone
2	0.25		
		Fine sand	Sandstone
3	0.125		
		Very fine sand	Sandstone
4	0.0625		
		Silt	Siltstone
8	0.0039		
		Clay	Claystone

The rather cumbersome particle diameter figures can be made easier to use by converting them to ϕ values (phi, pronounced in Britain like 'tie') by using the logarithm of the particle diameter. Using this system, a sandstone with a mean grain size of fine sand has a size range of 2 – 3ϕ rather than 0.25 – 0.125 mm. The ϕ system also makes the plotting of sediment size frequency diagrams more straightforward.

Mean grain size can only be measured by size analysis. Analysis is carried out most easily and effectively on loose sediment although there are methods that can be used on sedimentary rocks.

Loose sediment which is coarser than silt grade is most commonly analysed using sieving techniques. In this method a stack of sieves is used with decreasing mesh sizes from -2ϕ (4 mm holes) at the top to 4ϕ (0.0625 mm holes) at the base. The sieves may be at 1ϕ, $\frac{1}{2}\phi$ or $\frac{1}{4}\phi$ intervals. One hundred to two hundred grams of sediment are added to the top sieve and the whole stack is shaken for a fixed time (usually 20 minutes). Then the amount of sediment retained on each sieve is weighed and recorded. Coarse sediment of gravel grade can be analysed either by using coarser meshed sieves or by using rulers and tape measures. The latter method can be very time-consuming!

A second method of analysis, particularly good for finer grade sediments, is the sedimentation tube method. This is based upon the settling velocity of sediment particles in water. Coarse sediment settles to the bottom of a water column faster than fine sediment and so the different sediment fractions are separated by settling time. A settling tube is a broad glass tube, up to 2 metres high, filled with water. It has a device for measuring the weight of sediment that reaches the bottom after fixed time intervals. The sediment sample is introduced at the top and the amount of sediment which has accumulated at the base is measured at predetermined time intervals. This method gives results which can be reproduced, but is expensive and rather time-consuming as fine sediment takes many hours to settle.

After completion of the analysis, the results are plotted on **sediment size frequency diagrams**. The simplest plot is of size frequency against grain size which can be plotted either as a bar graph or as a curve, as shown in Figure 3.5 A. The whole figure shows five size frequency distributions for sediment samples from different environments. The distributions show that dune sand has a very small range of particle size and is therefore described as **well sorted**. Glacial till has a broad size range and so is **poorly sorted**. River sand has moderate sorting. If the sediments from two environments become mixed together then a two peaked (bimodal) plot may be produced.

The results can also be plotted on a cumulative frequency graph where the results for each size fraction are added in sequence. Figure 3.6 shows the examples from Figure 3.5, plotted on a cumulative frequency diagram. The advantage of this sort of graph is that several samples can be plotted on the same diagram and directly compared. In addition, the median grain size can be read from the plots very easily. Well-sorted sediments plot as steep, nearly straight lines, poorly sorted sediments have very curvaceous or low angle plots.

In ideal circumstances size frequency plots can be used directly to distinguish sediments from different environments; in reality there are many natural sediments that do not fit the 'ideal' plots, usually because the history of the sediment has been complicated. Because of these problems, geologists have tried to squeeze more information from size frequency results by calculating a measure of sorting in various ways. One popular method is to calculate the standard deviation, although other methods are also in common use. The shapes of the distribution curves can also be usefully analysed. These methods are useful in some circumstances but there are still natural sediments that do not fit the 'ideal' plots.

Mean grain size and sorting are difficult to analyse in consolidated sedimentary rocks. Some rocks can be broken down into loose sediment by ultrasonic vibration methods, but usually an assessment has to be carried out on solid rock. One way of tackling this problem is by using a thin section of the rock and measuring the sizes of randomly selected grains. However, a much simpler way, which can easily be applied in the field, is to use sediment size and sediment sorting comparators. Figure 3.7 shows how a sediment size comparator can be made of sieved sediment samples (it is useful to remember as well that silt can be distinguished from clay by the 'tooth test': silt is gritty, clay is not!). Figure 3.8 is a sediment sorting comparator. With a little experience, the mean grain size and sorting of a sedimentary rock can be gauged very accurately.

Figure 3.5
Sediment size frequency plots for sediment samples from different depositional environments.
How can river, beach and aeolian dune sands of the same mean grain size normally be distinguished from one another?

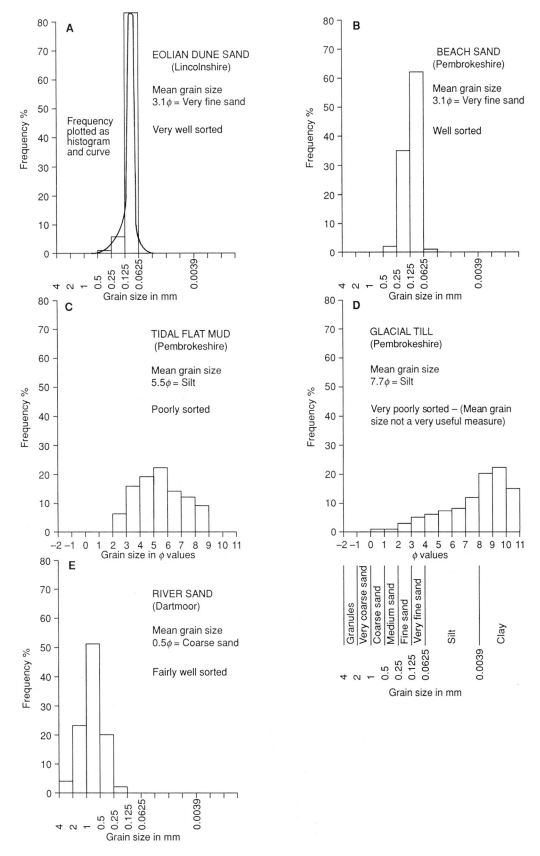

Figure 3.6
Cumulative sediment size frequency plots for the same samples as those plotted in Figure 3.4.
How can sediments with different sorting characteristics easily be distinguished using this type
of plot?

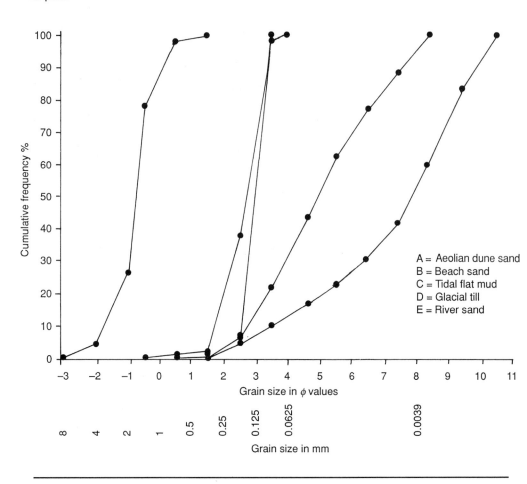

Figure 3.7
A sediment size comparator.
A very simple and cheap comparator can be made from part of a 30cm ruler by glueing sediment
of different grades into the central 'trough' of the ruler. The sediment grades must then be
labelled. What is the best technique to use to obtain sediment of the different grades required?

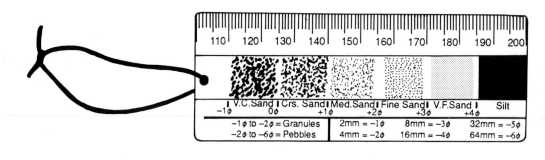

The size analysis methods used for clastic sedimentary rocks cannot be used for
limestones and other carbonate rocks because, during the rock-forming processes, the
carbonate particles can become greatly changed in size and shape. Thus only general
terms such as coarse-grained or fine-grained can be used for describing carbonate
sediments.

Figure 3.8
A sediment sorting comparator (after Compton, 1962; in Blatt, 1982).
Specimens should be examined through a hand lens (x 10) and compared with the chart. This sorting comparator can be glued to the base of the size comparator in Figure 3.7. How do the mean grain sizes of the sediments shown in the chart vary?

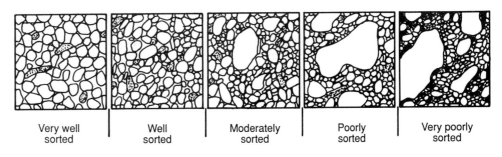

| Very well sorted | Well sorted | Moderately sorted | Poorly sorted | Very poorly sorted |

Figure 3.9
A classification system for limestones (after Dunham, 1962; in Tucker, 1982).
This system is based on limestone texture. What names are given to the following:
a) an oolithic limestone with less than 5% lime mud;
b) a bioclastic limestone with a lime mud matrix between the grains;
c) chalk?

Grainstone	*Packstone*	*Wackestone*	*Carbonate mudstone (or micrite)*	*Boundstone*
More than 95% grains	Less than 95% grains but mud only fills gaps between grains – grain supported	Less than 90% mud but grains are scattered and not in contact with one another – mud supported	More than 90% lime mud	Reef limestone
Mud content increasing ────────────────────────────────➤				
◀──────────────────────── Grain content increasing				

Nevertheless, the grain sizes of carbonates do provide important clues as to how they were formed. Bioclastic limestones formed from transported fossil fragments and shell debris are coarse-grained; ooidal limestones formed by strong evaporation of sea water in high energy conditions are also fairly coarse-grained. Fine lime mud is only deposited by evaporation or the breakdown of calcareous algae in very quiet lagoonal conditions. Various systems have been proposed for the classification of limestones. A useful one based on texture is that of Dunham, shown in Figure 3.9. Grainstones and packstones consist of grains, but mud can fill the pore spaces; in wackestones and mudstones the matrix is carbonate mud, but there can also be scattered grains such as shell fragments, ooids or pellets.

What Can Particle Size Analysis Tell Us?

The Dunham system of limestone classification, which is based upon texture, gives a good indication of the depositional environment, since grainstones and packstones form in high energy conditions and wackestones and carbonate mudstones in low energy conditions.

In the same way, coarse-grained clastic rocks such as conglomerates and coarse-grained sandstones can be deposited only in high energy conditions as found in fast flowing rivers, on beaches, etc. Fine-grained sediment is deposited in quiet conditions. Sediment produced by weathering and erosion usually has a broad range of particle size, but during transportation the particles become sorted. The further the transport, the more energy available for sorting and the better the sorting, in general. Thus poorly sorted sediments have been transported only short distances (or have been transported by a process that does not sort the sediments, e.g. by ice). Well-sorted sediments have travelled far or have been deposited in environments that naturally have a great deal of sorting energy available, such as wave-pounded beaches and wind-blown deserts.

Particle Shape

Analysis of Shape

Particle shape analysis is carried out on sand and gravel grade sediment but is not usually possible on finer grade material. Four main aspects of shape are commonly examined: **surface texture**, **form**, **sphericity** and **roundness**.

Physical weathering produces rock fragments with rough surface textures but these surfaces are soon smoothed off by attrition during transport. If the pebbles are thrown together during transport they may develop small crescent-shaped percussion marks. Pebbles transported by ice often have scratched or striated surfaces and sometimes the scratches can be in more than one direction. In deserts pebbles may develop shiny surfaces due to wind abrasion; this is called desert varnish. Desert sand grains usually have frosted surfaces whereas river sands have generally clean surfaces. Surface textures are changed during rock-forming processes and so the surfaces of particles in sedimentary rocks may not tell us very much about how they were formed.

Particle form is the overall shape of the particles and is usually described only for gravels and conglomerates. Particle shape is most commonly classified using Zingg's pebble classification system, shown in Figure 3.10. The length, breadth and thickness

Figure 3.10
A classification of pebble shapes (after Zingg, 1935; in Selley, 1976).
Measure the dimensions of various 'particles' found in a pencil case, such as rubbers and pencil sharpeners. Plot the results on the pebble shape diagram to find the particle shapes.

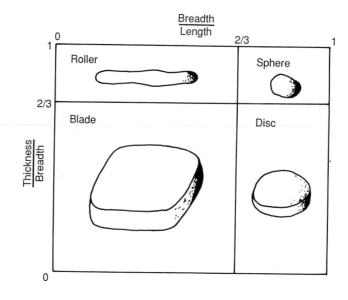

of each particle is measured, and the thickness:breadth ratio plotted against the breadth:length ratio. Rollers and spheres tend to roll during transport whereas discs and blades tend to slide. The shapes of pebbles are controlled largely by the weaknesses present in the parent rock: slates produce blades; massive rocks, like some limestones, produce more spherical particles.

The form of sand particles cannot be measured in the same way as pebbles and so the form is assessed by comparison with shapes of known sphericity. Sphericity is a measure of how close a particle shape is to that of a sphere or ball. Sand shapes vary from particles of very low sphericity, like mica flakes, to particles of high sphericity, like some desert sand grains. The sphericity of sand particles is largely controlled by crystal cleavage. Quartz with no cleavage tends to produce grains of fairly high sphericity.

The sphericity of grains is little changed by transport. A more useful shape property which is modified by transport is roundness. Roundness is a measure of the rounding of the corners of particles. While roundness can be measured and calculated, it is usually assessed by reference to shapes of standard roundness which range from angular – with sharp corners – to well-rounded – with no corners – as shown in Figure 3.11.

Scree particles are very angular and beach pebbles are usually well-rounded, due to the differences in their transportation histories.

Figure 3.11
Roundness and sphericity in sediment particles (after Tucker, 1982).
For each roundness category a grain of low and high sphericity is shown. Which is likely to have been transported further, an angular particle of high sphericity or a rounded particle of low sphericity?

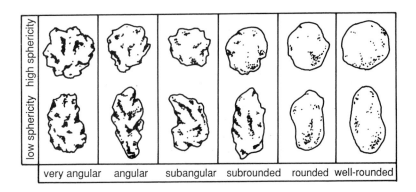

What Can Particle Shape Analysis Tell Us?

The overall shape (form and sphericity) of grains is controlled largely by weaknesses in the rock or crystals and so tells us little about the transport and depositional history of the sediment. Exceptions to this are the **ventifacts** (or **dreikanters**) which have one, two or three smooth surfaces and are produced in deserts by sand blasting. Some glacial pebbles have flattened and scratched bases due to attrition on bedrock during transport.

Rounding is a more useful property as it can give a guide to the history of the sediment: particles become progressively more rounded during transportation. Thus, angular grains cannot have travelled far. Desert sand grains are usually well-rounded, often with frosted surfaces, and frequently have a red coating of hematite as well.

Particle Orientation and Packing

Particle orientation and packing together determine the **fabric** of the sediment. Most sediment particles have one dimension longer than the others and the long axes are often orientated during the sedimentation process (try 'sedimenting' pencils on a wooden slope to find how their long axes orientate in relation to the dip of the slope). The importance of particle orientation is most obvious in some stream gravels where the long axes of the pebbles lie parallel to the stream flow direction and dip upstream. This feature is called **imbrication** and can be used to work out the flow directions of the currents which laid down ancient gravel deposits (see Figure 3.12). Beach gravels can also be imbricated but their imbrication directions are variable.

Figure 3.12
Imbrication.
An imbricated channel lag gravel shown in cartoon form. The clasts dip upstream. If imbricated stream gravels have a mean dip direction of 180° and a mean dip amount of 11°, in which direction was the current flowing?

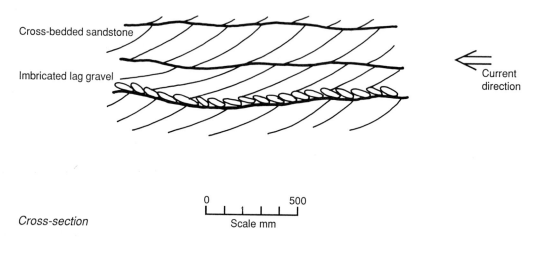

In rivers, sand grains tend to orientate themselves parallel to the flow direction and on beaches, parallel to the wave movement direction. However, grain orientation is difficult to determine in sandstones. Mica particles in sediments always orientate themselves with the flat surface down on the sediment bed, which is why micaceous sandstones split so easily parallel to the bedding.

Packing is the way in which the sediment particles are 'piled up' in a deposit. It is best to first consider the packing of 'ideal' particles which are spherical and of the same size, then to extend these ideas to real sediments.

Spheres can be packed by hand in the two ways shown in Figure 3.13. Cubic packing is the loosest possible type of packing and gives pore space of 48 per cent. Rhombohedral packing is the tightest possible configuration giving a pore space of 26 per cent. The rhombohedral packing is the more stable because each grain lies in a hollow in the grains beneath. If the loose particles are dropped one by one into a container, each grain finds its stable position and adopts a near rhombohedral packing configuration. However, if a handful of particles is dropped together, the grains interfere with each other and do not have time to adopt their most stable positions and the overall packing pattern tends towards cubic. Gently shaking the container causes the particles to repack themselves into a more stable configuration.

These 'ideal' spherical particles, being of one size only, have the best possible sorting. Real sediment is not spherical and is less well sorted, but with fairly well-sorted sand, slow deposition would tend to produce tight packing (similar to rhombohedral in ideal

Figure 3.13
The packing of spheres.
Cubic is the loosest possible packing, rhombohedral the tightest possible packing. If egg-shaped particles were packed in the same ways, would the porosities be higher or lower than for spherical particles?

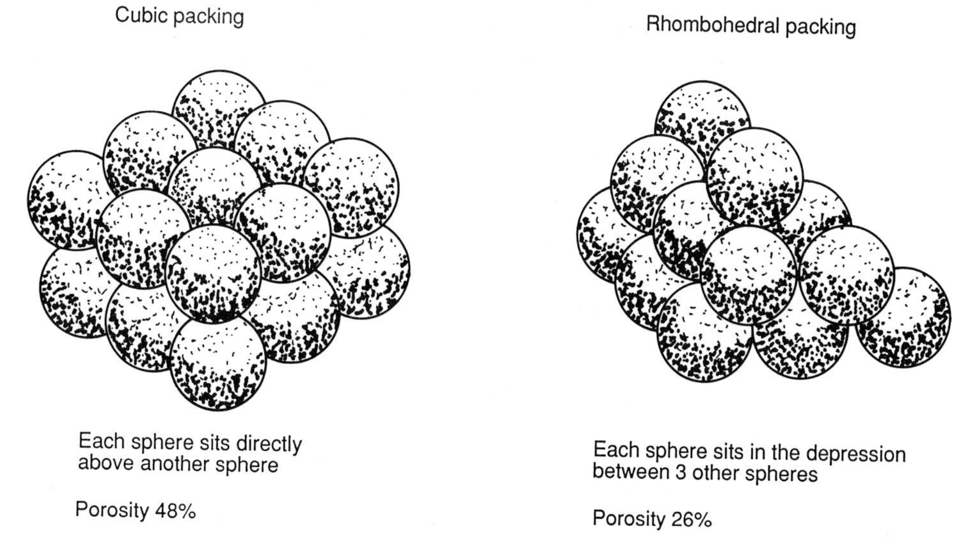

Cubic packing   Rhombohedral packing

Each sphere sits directly
above another sphere

Porosity 48%

Each sphere sits in the depression
between 3 other spheres

Porosity 26%

conditions) whereas fast deposition would produce looser packing. Therefore, sands that are deposited from slow-moving fluids tend to be tightly packed whereas sands that are deposited by collapsing down the faces of sand dunes are loosely packed.

In poorly sorted sediments, the spaces between the larger grains are filled with smaller grains and this has more effect on the porosity than the type of packing.

Porosity and Permeability

Porosity

Geologists are usually most interested in the particles of a sediment, but in applied geology the main interest often centres on the pores. This is because it is the pore spaces which can hold oil and gas, water for water supplies and deposits of hydrothermal minerals.

The amount of pore space in a rock is called the porosity and it is usually given as a percentage by using the following calculation:

$$\text{Porosity} = \frac{\text{volume of total pore space}}{\text{volume of rock sample}} \times 100$$

Two types of porosity are recognised. **Primary porosity** refers to the gaps between the particles, and forms during sedimentation. **Secondary porosity** is formed later by processes such as the recrystallisation or dissolving of minerals or by fracturing of the rock, etc. The amount of primary porosity depends upon textural features of the sediment, i.e. grain sorting, shape, orientation and packing.

Primary porosity can be measured by taking a cube or small core of rock, heating it to remove any water present and then, after weighing, placing the rock under water until it becomes saturated. A reweighing of the block (after surplus water has been 'mopped up') gives the weight of the water absorbed. The volume of the water, and thus the volume of the effective porosity in millilitres, is the same as the mass of the water in grams (since 1 ml of water weighs 1 gm). The **effective porosity** measured in this way is the volume of pore space which can be filled with fluid, which is the porosity in which the applied geologist is interested. The actual porosity is greater as there are pore spaces which the fluids cannot reach.

A good example of a rock with a fairly high primary porosity but a low effective porosity is a basalt containing gas holes or vesicles. Since the vesicles are not connected together, fluids cannot penetrate to those beneath the surface.

Primary porosities of larger bodies of rock are measured in the way described except that many rock samples may be tested in the lab and the results used for the overall calculation. Secondary porosity is more difficult to measure than primary porosity as the measurements have to be made on a large mass of rock.

Porosity can be measured indirectly in large rock masses by measuring the velocity of sound in the rock. Since the velocity of sound in water and in the rock particles is known, the ratio of water to rock can be calculated.

Porosity decreases with depth of burial of the sediment. This is because the more deeply it is buried, the greater is the pressure from the weight of rock above (the **overburden**) and so the more compacted the sediment becomes. Also, during burial and the rock-forming processes, new minerals grow in the pore spaces, further reducing porosity. As is shown in Figure 3.14, clay can initially have a very high porosity, but this is quickly lost with depth of burial. Sandstones initially have lower

Figure 3.14
The relationship between porosity and depth of burial of sediments (after Selley, 1976).
Why is clay generally less porous than sandstone at a depth of 2 km?

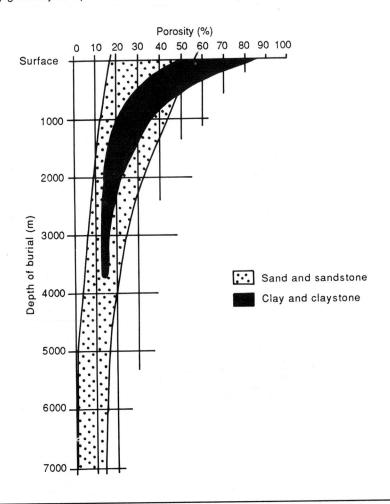

porosities but retain them to greater depths because they are more resistant to compaction. Even so, many sandstones lose their porosity as minerals grow in the pore spaces during cementation.

Permeability

The permeability of rocks is even more important to the applied geologist than the porosity. Permeability is a measure of how fast fluid can pass through a given rock. Rocks can have primary and secondary permeability in the same way as they have primary and secondary porosity. **Primary permeability** is the rate of fluid flow through pore spaces; **secondary permeability** is the rate of flow through secondary pores, cavities and fractures. Primary permeability can be measured in the lab but the apparatus is more complicated than that used for porosity measurements because the rate at which the fluid passes through the sample has to be measured. In rock sequences containing water, permeability can be measured by using pumping tests. These involve measuring the amount of water that can be pumped out of the well (borehole) in a given time, and then measuring how long the water takes to rise back to its original level in the well. The permeability of oil and gas reservoir rocks can be measured in a similar way. Secondary permeability is much greater when flow is parallel to joint and fracture trends than when across these trends.

The permeability of a rock depends not only on its effective porosity but also on the size of the pore spaces. If the pores are very small, as in clay, the fluid cannot flow through. Thus clay is **impermeable**. This is despite the fact that clay can hold large quantities of fluids (up to 80 per cent) and so is very porous. In general, however, non-porous rocks and very fine-grained rocks are impermeable, medium-grain-sized and poorly-sorted sedimentary rocks have moderate permeability and coarse-grained, well-sorted rocks have high permeability, as is shown in Figure 3.15. Thus it is the

---

Figure 3.15
Thin sections seen through the microscope to show porosity–permeability differences.
Rank the rock types shown in order of potential for oil or water reservoir rocks.

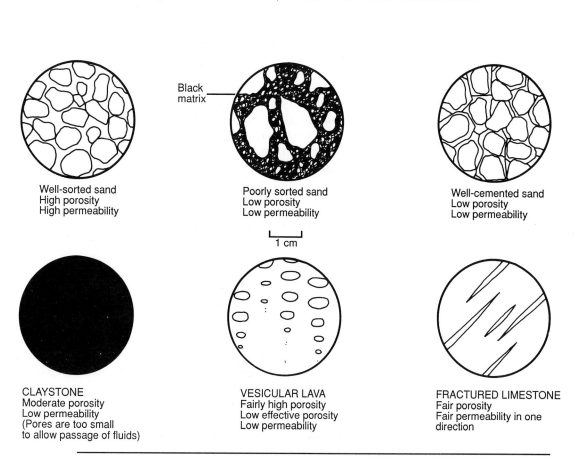

Well-sorted sand
High porosity
High permeability

Black matrix

Poorly sorted sand
Low porosity
Low permeability

1 cm

Well-cemented sand
Low porosity
Low permeability

CLAYSTONE
Moderate porosity
Low permeability
(Pores are too small
to allow passage of fluids)

VESICULAR LAVA
Fairly high porosity
Low effective porosity
Low permeability

FRACTURED LIMESTONE
Fair porosity
Fair permeability in one
direction

coarse-grained, well-sorted sediments that make the best oil and water reservoir rocks. There can be problems even when this type of rock is found by prospecting because cement may have been deposited in the pore spaces, greatly reducing permeability. This is why good reservoir rocks are not found very often!

Analysing Sediment in Boreholes

When geologists need to discover the detailed characteristics of the sedimentary rocks beneath their feet it becomes necessary either to bring the rocks to the surface, or to go down to the rocks. If the rocks are near the surface, they can be reached by digging trenches or pits; if they are situated at a deeper level and are on the site of previous mine excavations, they can be sampled from underground exposures; in any other circumstances the rocks can be reached only by drilling **boreholes**. Boreholes are round holes which can be bored by a number of different types of drill for a variety of purposes. For example, boreholes in sedimentary rocks are used in prospecting for water, coal, oil and gas, minerals etc. and also for **geotechnical work** where the foundation rocks beneath new structures such as buildings, roads, bridges and dams, have to be checked for strength and other properties.

More information can be gained from these holes if **cores** are extracted. Cores are cylindrical pieces of rock recovered from the centre of a hole. They are very valuable because they are examples of the rock, just as it is found beneath the surface, which can be observed and tested in the lab. Unfortunately, cores are very expensive to drill and recover for a large number of reasons. In weak rocks, it may be impossible to recover them at all. Thus many boreholes are not cored. Instead, the rock in the hole is completely broken up, by rotating the drill bit, and brought to the surface as rock chippings. These too can be very useful and give a good indication of the rock type and the microfossils found at depth. The chippings can, however, be contaminated by pieces of rock from higher up the borehole and it can be difficult to know the exact depth from which they come.

Drilling boreholes is expensive. Geologists want to gain as much information from them as possible. Because of the problems associated with coring and using rock chippings, modern 'high-technology' methods of analysis are now being used. After the hole has been drilled, a series of measuring devices contained in a cylindrical capsule called a **sonde** are lowered down the hole on a **wireline** (an armoured electrical cable). As the sonde is slowly pulled up the hole, measurements are made and transmitted to the surface, where they are recorded. The whole process is known as **downhole logging** and one of its major values is that it shows the exact depth at which changes in the rock sequence occur. It is now possible to make a large number of measurements in this way and some of the more important of these are summarised in the paragraphs below.

Caliper Measurements
The caliper simply measures the width of the hole. The softer the rock, the greater the diameter of the hole. The geologist will already have a fair idea about the rock hardness because softer rocks can be drilled much faster than hard rocks, and drillers are expert at interpreting drilling rate data, but the caliper measurements will be used to confirm the drilling rate observations and to give the exact depths of the changes. The type of plot produced by a caliper, and by other measuring instruments, is shown in Figure 3.16.

Gamma Rays
Many rocks naturally emit gamma rays and this natural emission can be measured. Most of the gamma radiation is emitted by radioactive decay of the potassium found in some minerals. Clays and shales contain more potassium-rich minerals than do sandstones and so a sudden increase in gamma radiation often signals that the sonde has passed from sandstone into clay or shale.

Figure 3.16
Generalised logs produced by the downhole logging of a borehole drilled through the sequences shown.
Which particular features give clues to:
a) the presence of hydrocarbons; b) the presence of coal?

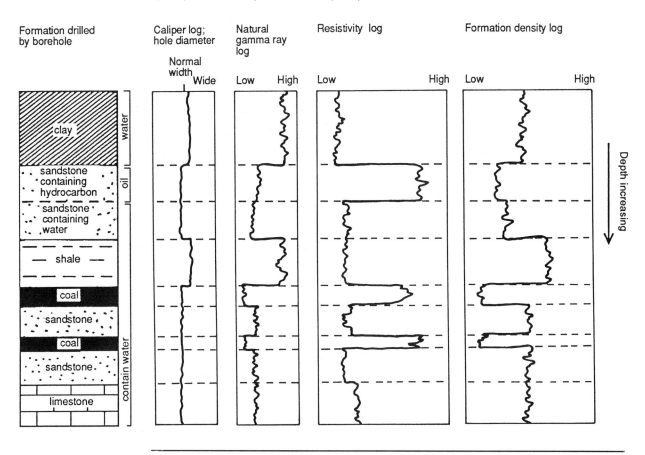

The presence of **hydrocarbon source rocks** (i.e. the rocks from which oil and gas originally came) can also be indicated by gamma radiation measurements, since the rocks usually contain uranium which also breaks down radioactively producing gamma rays.

Resistivity

If rocks conduct electricity well, they have a low resistivity; if they are poor conductors, they have a high resistivity. In fact, rocks themselves hardly conduct electricity at all: it is the water within the pore spaces which, when it is rich in ions, can conduct electricity relatively well. Thus a rock which has low resistivity must contain a lot of water and must therefore be porous, e.g. a porous sandstone. Rocks like granite have no pore spaces which can contain water and thus have a very high resistivity. Resistivity measurements therefore give a good indication of rock porosity.

In prospecting for oil and gas, knowledge of rock porosity is vital. High resistivity measurements can also indicate the presence of hydrocarbons, because oil and gas are very bad conductors of electricity. Thus, if there is a sudden increase in resistivity without a change in rock type, the sonde may have passed from a porous rock filled with water to one filled with hydrocarbon.

Resistivity measurements can also be useful when prospecting for coal, as coal seams have a high resistivity in comparison with the rocks that usually occur above and below them.

Formation Density

A good guide to the density of the rocks being studied can be gained by firing radiation at the rock in the borehole and measuring how much is reflected. The denser the rock, the more radiation will be reflected. This is a good method for finding coal since the coal has lower densities than the surrounding rocks. The formation density measurement is another indication of rock porosity since porous rocks have lower densities than rocks with low porosity.

The information gained by the high-tech methods discussed above is summarised in Figure 3.17 with regard to a selection of important rocks.

Figure 3.17
A summary of the information on certain rock types that can be gained by downhole logging techniques.
Individual rock types can have very variable properties and responses to the different techniques; thus only a general guide showing relative values can be given. How can the differences between porous and non-porous sandstone be explained?

Type of Formation	Caliper Diameter of Hole	Gamma Ray	Resistivity	Formation Density
Clay or shale	Wide	High	Very low	High
Porous sandstone with water	Normal	Low	Low	Low
Porous sandstone with hydrocarbon	Normal	Low	High	Low
Impermeable (non-porous) sandstone	Normal	Low	High	High
Oil shale (hydrocarbon source rock)	Wide	High	Low	High
Coal	Normal	Very low	High	Very low

Several other high-tech methods have been developed to measure the properties of the rock down a borehole. These include techniques to measure the velocity of sound waves passing through the rock, and the effects on the rock of neutron bombardment. It is also possible to extract small cores of rock by 'firing' short cylinders into the side of the hole to 'see' the rock in place. The modern prospector, therefore, tends to spend much more time studying computer print-outs and small rock fragments, and much less time examining rocks in the field.

Economic Aspects

Underground Water Supply

More than 25 per cent of the water used in England and Wales comes from underground reservoir rocks. These permeable rocks are called **aquifers** and receive their water from rainfall and streams, lakes, etc. The surface water **infiltrates** (flows downwards) through the soil and bedrock until it reaches the depth where the pores are filled (or **saturated**) with water. The top of this **zone of saturation** is called the **water table**. The water table is not a flat surface but undulates as a subdued reflection of the surface relief. Where the water table is at the level of the ground surface, water comes out of the ground forming springs or marshy areas, as shown in Figure 3.18.

Figure 3.18
The water table, the top surface of the zone of saturation.
Water infiltrates down to the water table and then percolates down the slope of the water table in groundwater flow. Where the water table cuts the surface, water comes out of the ground forming springs or adding to streams, etc. Where water is held up by an impermeable bed, a perched water table is formed. Where, on the diagram, would be the best place to drill a water well? What causes the level of the water table to move up and down?

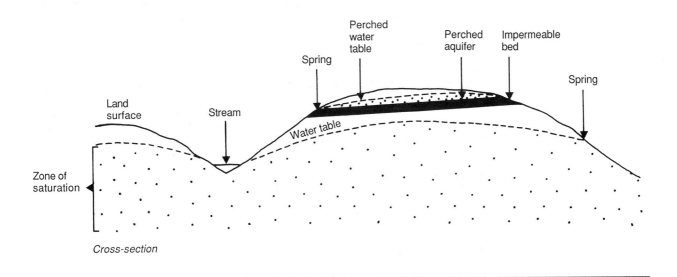

Cross-section

All the water that lies beneath the water table is called **groundwater**. Groundwater is **abstracted** (extracted) by drilling boreholes, called wells, to beneath the water table and then pumping the water to the surface. If the well is successful, then groundwater will flow through the permeable rock and into the borehole at the same rate as it is being pumped to the surface. If not, then the **cone of depression** caused by the pumping (see Figure 3.19) will fall below the bottom of the borehole so that no water can enter the well until the pumping ceases. This is called **overpumping** of the well. Pumping wells cannot be too close together otherwise the two cones of depression will meet and either the rates of pumping will have to be reduced or overpumping will occur.

The chalk aquifer beneath London has been overpumped for years and this has not only caused some wells to become dry but also, where the water has been removed, the chalk particles are no longer supported by the water, allowing the chalk to become more compacted. This has contributed to the slow sinking of the London area which has increased the risk of flooding and made the Thames barrier, built to stop the flooding of the city, even more necessary. Overpumping is also contributing to the steady subsidence of the famous Italian city of Venice into the sea.

Some recent attempts to **recharge** the chalk aquifer beneath London by pumping water into the rock have been fairly successful but they can never reverse the chalk compaction that has already occurred.

Where an aquifer dips and has impermeable beds like clay above and below, an **artesian** groundwater supply can be formed (see Figure 3.20). The groundwater in the basin is under pressure from the head of water in the surrounding hills and so when a well is drilled into the aquifer the water squirts upwards. If the water reaches the surface a flowing artesian well is formed. The water supplies from the London chalk aquifer used to be artesian before overpumping. Artesian water supplies are very important in some of the dry interior areas of central Australia.

Figure 3.19
Pumping wells and overpumping.
How can overpumping of wells be avoided? What will happen to the water table when pumping ceases?

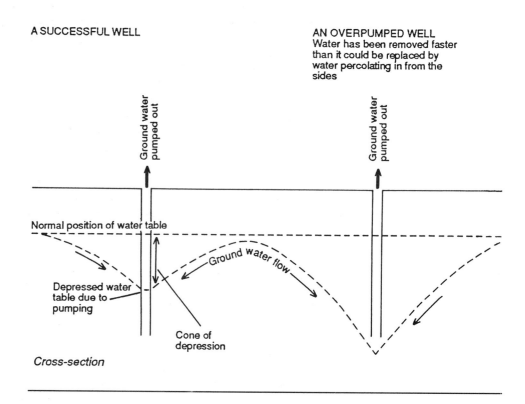

A SUCCESSFUL WELL

AN OVERPUMPED WELL
Water has been removed faster than it could be replaced by water percolating in from the sides

Ground water pumped out

Ground water pumped out

Normal position of water table

Ground water flow

Depressed water table due to pumping

Cone of depression

Cross-section

Figure 3.20
Artesian water.
When an aquifer dips below the surface and has impermeable beds above and below, it becomes confined. Wells drilled to the confined aquifer produce artesian water which can flow freely from the well if the top of the well is below the level of the water table which would be present if the aquifer were unconfined. Why is artesian water often rich in dissolved mineral salts?

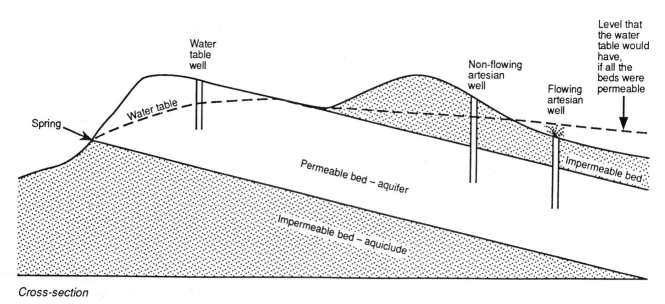

Water table well

Non-flowing artesian well

Level that the water table would have, if all the beds were permeable

Flowing artesian well

Spring

Water table

Permeable bed – aquifer

Impermeable bed

Impermeable bed – aquiclude

Cross-section

Siting Water Reservoirs

When a water reservoir is being planned, many factors have to be taken into consideration. These include the amount of rainfall, the valley shape, the size of the dam necessary, the sources of material available to build the dam, the reaction of the local people and the authorities, the distance of the reservoir from where the water is needed, etc. However, even if all these factors are favourable, the reservoir cannot be created if the bedrock is unsuitable. The underlying rock must be strong enough to support the dam but must also be impermeable. A permeable bedrock will allow water to percolate away and be lost. If only a part of the area to be flooded has permeable bedrock, then this can be lined with impermeable clay, but it is an expensive operation.

Oil and Gas Reservoir Rocks

Water moves down into rocks but natural gas and oil migrate upwards through permeable rocks as they are less dense than the groundwater within the rocks. Four factors are necessary to produce an exploitable oil reservoir: a **source** of hydrocarbon fluid (such as an oil shale or a coal); a **reservoir rock** (with enough permeability to store large quantities of oil or gas); a **cap rock** (an impermeable rock which will trap the hydrocarbon by stopping its upward migration); and a **trap** (a structural or stratigraphic feature which traps the hydrocarbon underground like a bubble). Some possible oil and gas reservoir situations are shown in Figure 3.21.

The oil and gas reservoirs of the North Sea are of a variety of types and ages. They include limestones and sandstones of several geological periods from Devonian to Tertiary. The oil reservoirs of the North Sea have made Britain self-sufficient in oil, but at present production levels they will last for only another 30 to 40 years.

Hydrothermal Mineral Deposits

Hydrothermal mineral deposits form from hot waters that rise from heat sources deep within the crust. Many different types of minerals are deposited by such hydrothermal fluids, including cassiterite (tin ore), chalcopyrite (copper ore), galena (lead ore), sphalerite (zinc ore) and several iron ores. The heat sources producing the hydrothermal fluids are often igneous intrusions such as granites, but may be areas that are undergoing regional metamorphism. The hot waters involved are either **juvenile** waters, that is, 'new' water formed during the cooling of the magma, or **meteoric** water. Meteoric water is 'rain' water that has infiltrated into the ground to become groundwater. Groundwater near the heat source rises and new groundwater circulates down to replace it, producing a water convection cell. **Connate** water, or water buried with the original sediments, may also be involved.

These waters are not strictly waters at all, but are brines. The brines form because the intense pressures and high temperatures at depth make the waters into very powerful solvents, capable of dissolving large quantities of a variety of minerals.

The brines rise to the surface above the heat source through the natural porosity of the rock. As they rise they cool, causing some of the dissolved salts to precipitate onto the walls of the pores through which they are flowing. If the flow channels are joints and fractures, **mineral veins** form. If the flow is through the angular breccias formed along some faults, **mineralised fault breccias** form. If the fluids pass through the primary pore spaces of the rock, then a **disseminated ore deposit** forms with the minerals being dispersed through the pore spaces. These three types of hydrothermal ore deposits are shown in Figure 3.22.

In the case of disseminated ore deposits in sedimentary rocks, the fluids flow along particularly permeable beds and deposits, so sandstone beds which are rich in ores can be sandwiched between other beds which are poor in ores. Sometimes 'cap rocks' have the same importance as in gas and oil reservoirs, stopping the upward migration of the brines. The trapped brines then cool, precipitating minerals in veins and pore spaces beneath the impermeable cap of clay, shale, etc. The control of the mineralisation by the permeability of the rock can be seen clearly in some of the lead-fluorite deposits of the Peak District and the lead-copper-barite deposits of the Alderley Edge area of north Cheshire.

Figure 3.21
Possible oil and gas traps shown in diagrammatic form.
The hydrocarbons percolate upwards through paths not shown on the diagram until they are trapped in permeable reservoir rocks beneath impermeable cap rocks. Water is always found below the oil in traps. When oil and gas are found together, why is the gas always above the oil? How could the oil and gas become separated?

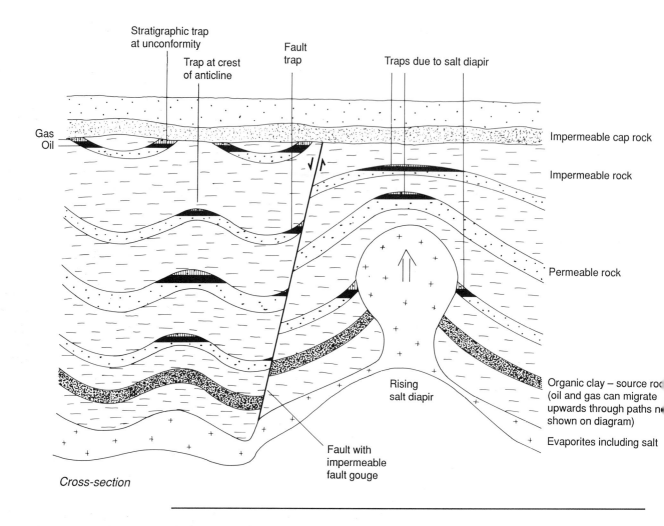

Hydrothermal fluids flowing along faults and joints have frequently penetrated the pores of the wall rock on either side, causing great rock alteration as well as mineral crystallisation. The chemistry of fluids changes during crystallisation, as is evidenced by the fact that veins are often found which have sequences of minerals that grew in from the walls on either side, forming mirror-image banding, as shown in Figure 3.23.

Disposal of Toxic Chemical and Radioactive Waste
Some industrial chemical processes produce waste materials that are highly poisonous and which therefore need to be disposed of in places that are as safe as possible. The most obvious place to dump large quantities of these chemicals is in abandoned quarries, but this can be highly dangerous if the quarry rocks are permeable. Permeable rocks will allow circulating groundwater to rot the containers of the chemicals and take the waste materials into the groundwater flow. The polluted groundwater may eventually reach streams or rivers or be pumped out of aquifers for our water supply. Thus, very careful surveys of the hydrogeology of the quarry must be carried out before any dumping of toxic wastes takes place.

Figure 3.22
Sites of possible hydrothermal ore deposits shown in diagrammatic form.
Hydrothermal fluids rich in dissolved minerals rise through fractures and permeable rocks, cooling and causing minerals to be deposited. Which minerals will be first to crystallise in the veins: ones that crystallise at high temperatures, or the low temperature minerals?

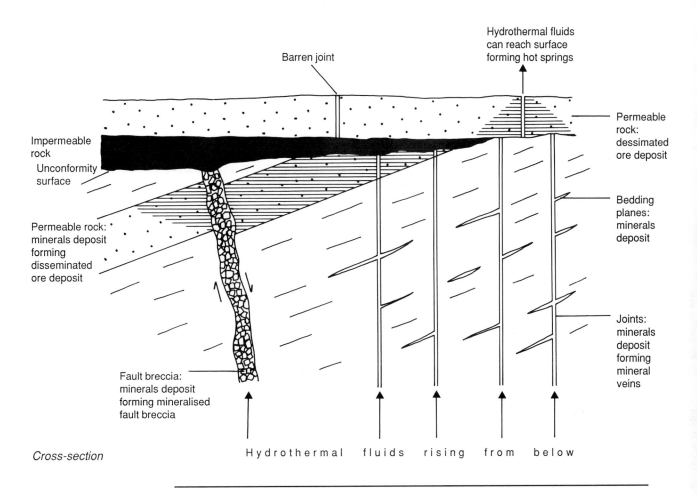

Hydrothermal fluids can reach surface forming hot springs

Barren joint

Permeable rock: dessimated ore deposit

Impermeable rock

Unconformity surface

Permeable rock: minerals deposit forming disseminated ore deposit

Bedding planes: minerals deposit

Joints: minerals deposit forming mineral veins

Fault breccia: minerals deposit forming mineralised fault breccia

Cross-section   H y d r o t h e r m a l   f l u i d s   r i s i n g   f r o m   b e l o w

Figure 3.23
Mineral veins containing different minerals.
Sequences of minerals growing in from the vein walls indicate that the rising hydrothermal fluids changed during crystallisation. What were the mineral crystallisation sequences in the veins shown?

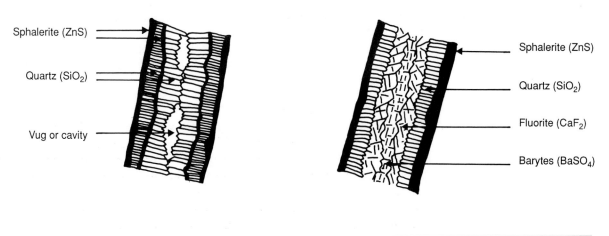

Sphalerite (ZnS)

Quartz (SiO_2)

Vug or cavity

Sphalerite (ZnS)

Quartz (SiO_2)

Fluorite (CaF_2)

Barytes ($BaSO_4$)

The conditions for the disposal of radioactive waste are even more stringent because some dangerous radioactive materials do not decay to harmless levels for thousands, sometimes millions, of years. Disposal must therefore be safe for that length of time. The waste must be disposed of in rocks that are not only very impermeable, but are also unlikely to fracture during earthquake activity. Many different types of rock have been examined for these properties and the most suitable are thick clay deposits, evaporite (mainly rock salt) deposits and granite intrusions. The evaporite and clay deposits have the advantage of being easy to excavate and the property of flowing plastically to close any fractures that might form. Granites have the advantage of occurring in very stable areas and usually have low permeability. Other suggestions for radioactive waste disposal, for example in deep ocean trenches or in polar ice caps, have proved to be more impractical or expensive, at the present time, than the bedrock option.

Practical Investigation and Fieldwork

By carrying out the following investigations, you will deepen your understanding of the principles described in this chapter.

1. How do pebbles from different environments differ?
Take small, randomly selected pebbles from a beach, a river and a scree. Measure their dimensions and plot the results on a Zingg pebble shape diagram (as in Figure 3.10). Estimate their angularity–roundness by referring to Figure 3.11. Describe the differences in surface texture. How can these properties be used to understand the depositional environments of ancient gravels?

2. How do sands from different environments differ?
Use a binocular microscope or a hand lens to examine samples of beach, dune and river sand. How do the compositions of the samples compare? How do the grain shapes vary in terms of angularity-roundness and sphericity? Can these variations be used to distinguish sand deposits from ancient beaches, dunes and rivers?

3. What is the grain size distribution of a sand sample, analysed by the sieving method?
Do a sieve analysis by the method described on page 46. First assemble the sieve stack with the sieves in the correct sequence, largest mesh at the top. Take a suitable quantity of dry sand (e.g. 60 – 80 gm) and add to the top of the sieve stack. Shake the stack vigorously for 10 minutes using up and down and round and round movements. Weigh the coarsest fraction and record the result. Add the next coarsest and weigh again, recording the result. Repeat this for all the fractions (this weighing method reduces errors). The weights you have recorded can be plotted directly to give a cumulative sediment size frequency plot like the ones in Figure 3.6. The weights of each fraction can be found by subtraction from the cumulative results, and should be plotted as in Figure 3.5. If you compare your results with the plots of these two figures you may be able to decide what type of environment your sand sample came from.

4. What is the grain size distribution of a sand sample, analysed by the settling tube method?
Take a school burette, close the tap and fill with sand up to the bottom graduation (50 ml), then carefully fill the burette with water to near the top. If you have sieved sediment available, calibrate the settling tube yourself by timing the fall of all grades of sediment from granule grade to coarse silt grade. If there is no sieved sediment available, then the calibration times shown in Figure 3.24 are a good guide. Place a small sand sample in a small funnel and wash the sediment into the burette as you start the stop-watch. Record the depth of sediment at the bottom, at the times you calculated or at those given in Figure 3.24. Plot the results either as a cumulative sediment size frequency curve (Figure 3.6) or, by subtraction, as a bar graph (Figure 3.5). From what environment is your sand sample most likely to have come? (This experiment was first described by Bateman *et al.*, 1983.)

Figure 3.24
Calibration for a 50 ml burette used as a settling tube.
The calibration is given as a table and in graph form. This calibration can be used in the measurement of sediment size distributions in any 50 ml burette. How would the calibration change if the burette were only half full of water?

Grain size		Settling time (seconds)
Sediment grade	ϕ Values	
		0
Granule	−2 - 1	3.8
Very coarse sand	−1 - 0	4.8
Coarse sand	0 - 1	12.2
Medium sand	1 - 2	36.0
Fine sand	2 - 3	88.1
Very fine sand	3 - 4	141.0
Silt	> 4	451.0

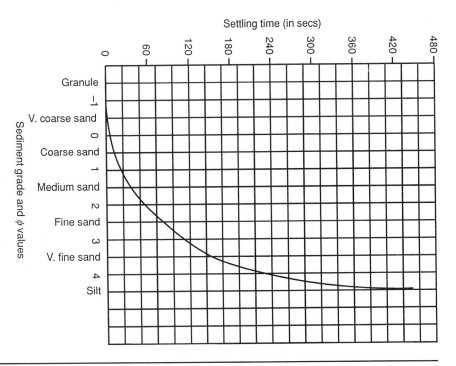

5. How does the packing of 'ideal' sedimentary particles affect their porosity?
Take 16 polystyrene balls of the type frequently used in chemistry departments to make atomic models. Cut four of the particles carefully in half. Make a cardboard box with a square base that is open at the top – the base should be two ball diameters square and the sides three ball diameters high. Pack the whole balls into the box with a cubic packing arrangement, i.e. with each ball sitting on top of the one below. Calculate the volume of the box in millilitres (length x breadth x height in mm). Calculate the volume of the particles, by finding the volume of one particle ($4/3\pi r^3$, r=radius), and multiplying this by the number of particles. Then calculate the porosity using the following formula:

$$\frac{\text{volume of box - volume of particles}}{\text{volume of box}} \times 100\%$$

Repeat the experiment, but using rhombohedral packing, i.e. to make the second layer, place a particle in the centre of the four particles at the base of the box and fill the surrounding spaces with half particles; the third layer is a repeat of the first layer, etc. Measure the volume of space occupied by the particles and the number of particles and repeat the calculation. Which packing system is the tighter? Which gives the higher porosity? Why are the porosity figures obtained in your investigation different from those given on page 54?

6. How do the different processes of sand sedimentation affect the packing and porosity of the sediments produced?
Take a sample of dune sand and pour it into a beaker (sand collapsing down the front of a dune sediments itself in this way). Gently flatten the sediment surface and record its height on the side of the beaker. Gently tap the beaker to resediment the sand in a more stable configuration. Observe the new level of sand. How do the levels differ? Measure and compare the porosities directly. Carefully add water to the 'poured in' sand sample until it reaches the sand surface. Find the amount of water added, either by careful measurement during pouring, or by weighing the beaker before and after

adding the water. Repeat the measurement after 'tapping' and removing the surplus water by placing thin card on the sand and pouring the water off. Then calculate the porosities using the following formula:

$$\frac{\text{volume of water}}{\text{volume of beaker occupied by sediment}} \times 100\%$$

(volume of beaker occupied by sediment = $\pi r^2 \times$ height of sediment; r = radius of beaker)

Why do the measured porosities differ?

7. How do the effective porosities of different rock types differ?
Carry out the experiment described on page 53 for various fairly porous rock types. What range of effective porosities do natural rocks have?

(Investigations 5, 6 and 7 were first described by Thompson, 1979.)

8. How does the permeability of loose sediment vary with grain size?
Set up a series of vertical tubes of about 15 mm diameter which are closed at the bottom with rubber tubing and a clip. Place a small plug of cotton wool at the base of each tube and half fill each one with sieved sediment of various grades, from granule to very fine sand. Pour a measured volume of water into each tube, enough to fill the tube nearly to the top. Release the clips and measure the time taken for 75 per cent of the water to drain from the samples. Calculate the water discharge rates in ml sec^{-1}. Plot the results on a graph of discharge against grain size. Is the plot a smooth curve? Why does it have the shape plotted? (This experiment was first demonstrated by Thompson, 1979.)

Test Your Understanding

1. Use a table like the one shown below to describe the sand types you might expect to find in the following depositional environments: stream near source; river near mouth; beach; aeolian sand dune.

Sand Sample from:	Mineralogical Composition	Sorting	Texture Roundness-Angularity	Packing

2. A series of sediment samples was taken from various places along a river bed as follows:

a) near the source;
b) downstream of a confluence between two tributaries;
c) in the middle reaches of the river;
d) on the coastal plain;
e) in the muddy estuary.

Draw the sediment size distribution curve or bar chart you would expect for each sample.

3. In some desert areas the sand dunes are composed of well-sorted fine and medium grade sands whereas the desert floor between the dunes is composed of coarse sand and very fine sediment together. How could the bimodal desert floor sediment have been produced?

4. Physical weathering produces fragments of the following rock types: slate; massive limestone; shale with ironstone nodules; well-bedded sandstone. How would you expect the particle shapes to differ?

5. In Louisiana, USA, beds of Tertiary sand dip from near the surface to a depth of 6 km. Their porosity changes from 36 per cent near the surface to 20 per cent at 6 km depth. What two factors could have caused this change in porosity?

6. A dry valley passes down the flank of Ingleborough in the western Yorkshire Dales. Low down in the valley a spring emerges forming the source of Jenkin's Beck. In the winter the water emerges slightly higher up the valley than in the summer. Why? What effect would you expect a sudden summer storm to have on the situation?

7. Figure 3.25 shows part of a downhole log through a sandstone/shale sequence that contains hydrocarbons. How many beds of sandstone are contained in this sequence? Between which depths might you expect to find oil and/or gas?

8. During a coal prospecting programme carried out in Staffordshire, boreholes were drilled through a Carboniferous sandstone/shale sequence and seams of coal were found. How might different formations of sandstone and shale and seams of coal be recognised by downhole logging techniques?

Figure 3.25
Downhole logs that might be produced in a sequence of sandstones and shales containing hydrocarbons.
In which ways do the information given by downhole logging and the information given from examination of borehole rock chippings differ?

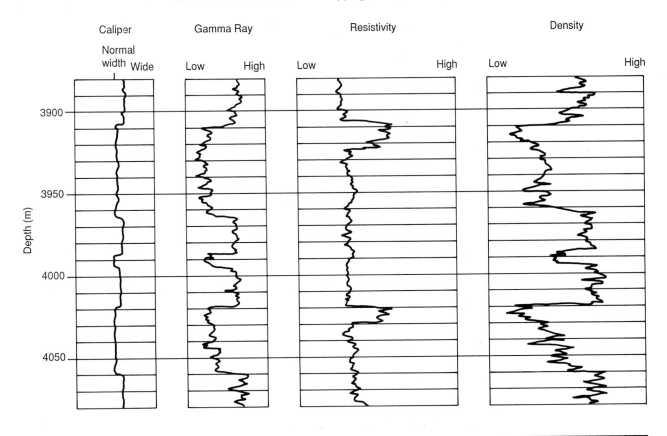

4. WHAT CAN THE SEDIMENT BODY TELL US?

Analysing the Sediment Body

The Sediment Body

All the sediments formed and laid down in a modern sedimentary environment together make up the **sediment body**. The sediments may have been transported into the area, formed within it, or both. The sediment body of a delta for example, will have a top, a front and a bottom, and will contain gravels, sands and muds laid down in a variety of ways with a variety of structures. The organisms that lived and died there will also have had important effects on the sediment. All this activity produces a sediment body whose shape and sequence are likely to be similar to those of other deltas and thus are characteristic of delta environments. If a similar shape and sediment sequence is recognised preserved in ancient rocks, then the sediment body is likely to have been deposited as a delta back in distant geological time. As some delta sequences contain oil, so an ancient delta sequence may have important economic potential for today.

As well as examining the sediments in detail, the sedimentary geologist therefore must also consider the sediment body as a whole. The headings A–G below help in the analysis and discussion of sediment bodies.

Analysing the Sediment Body

A. Conditions of Initiation

The initiation of **depositional environments**, the environments in which sediments are laid down and preserved, must always be triggered by a certain set of conditions. When studying modern depositional environments, these necessary 'triggers' or conditions of initiation must be identified. Many of these are obvious: for example, glacial environments cannot occur unless temperatures are less than 0°C (for at least the majority of the time), and deep sea sedimentation can only occur in the quiet, stable conditions of deep oceans. Other conditions of initiation, however, are less obvious: for example, one of the triggers for reef formation in shallow seas is an absence of mud from outside sources, because the necessary prolific life cannot flourish in murky seas.

Often there are a number of conditions of initiation. Reefs, for example, need the following: clear water (as explained above); shallow water (for light to penetrate and for water movement to bring food and oxygen); normal marine conditions (reef organisms cannot survive in fresh, brackish or very salt water); warm conditions (growth of the organisms and their food supply is only fast enough under tropical and sub-tropical conditions).

B. Transportation and Deposition

If the depositional environment of an ancient rock sequence is to be understood in detail, then one of the necessary investigations must be on the processes active in similar modern environments. The geologist must study the processes of sediment formation, movement and deposition within the sedimentary environment and link these to the types of sediment and different forms of sedimentary structures produced. Transportation and deposition can be studied, not only where these processes are happening in various places on Earth today, but also in the lab (as shown in Chapter 2). Lab experiments are used to recreate depositional environments in a controlled way, where the different factors involved can be more easily observed, measured and varied to find out how nature works in detail.

C. Sediment Types

Frequently, it is the types of sediment involved that give the first clues to the environment of deposition of an ancient rock sequence. Study of sediment type involves the consideration of sediment composition, shape, size, and the other properties which were dealt with in Chapter 3. Even the variability of sediment can be an important factor in interpretation: for example, sand dunes formed by wind contain only well-sorted sand, whereas lakes near the margins of ice sheets may hold a wide variety of sediments produced by a number of processes and sources.

D. Sedimentary Structures

While the types of sediment present often give the first clues to the original depositional environment, it is usually through analysis of the sedimentary structures, or the flora and fauna, or both together, that detailed understanding of ancient depositional conditions is reached. The structures involved range from the common bedding and lamination (which usually indicate that sediment was laid down in water), to symmetrical ripples (produced only by waves), to desiccation cracks (normally formed only when mud deposited by water dries out), to sole structures (generally formed only by fast-flowing turbidity currents). All these structures provide critical evidence about the environment of deposition; some of them can be used to provide more information about the palaeogeography of the depositional area through palaeocurrent analysis, a process which is described below.

Palaeocurrent analysis

Some sedimentary structures can be used to determine the direction of movement of the transporting agent (water, wind or ice) that formed them. Other structures that are symmetrical (e.g. grooves or symmetrical ripples) indicate only the trend of movement (i.e. a north–south trending groove scratched by a glacier on bedrock could have been formed by the ice moving from north to south, or from south to north). The most useful structures for these investigations are listed in the table, Figure 4.1.

Since the transporting agents form sedimentary structures that 'fan around' the mean direction of movement, palaeocurrent analysis involves making fairly large numbers of measurements. These are then plotted on a rose diagram which shows the amount of 'fanning' and gives a guide to the overall current direction. The mean current direction may be calculated and then also plotted on the diagram. The types of result that might be expected are plotted in Figure 4.2.

E. Fauna and Flora

The range and number of different species present in sediment, their positions therein and the method and state of their preservation can provide extremely valuable evidence in the interpretation of sedimentary sequences. Where life was abundant and its remains are well preserved in the sediment, the correct conditions of energy, light, salinity, food supply, temperature, etc., must have been present as the sediment body was building up. Sediments without any fossils must have formed in one of three ways: either they formed before life existed in that environment; or they did so in conditions too hostile for life to exist there; or living things were originally present, but they did not survive the processes of fossilisation.

Figure 4.1
Structures that can be used to give the movement directions of the agents that formed them.
Why can some structures give only a trend of movement while others can give a direction of
movement?

Sedimentary Structure	Agent of Formation	Indication
Small-scale cross bedding (less than 1 m sets)	Water currents	Direction of flow
Large-scale cross bedding (greater than 1 m sets)	Wind currents	Direction of flow
Asymmetrical ripples	Water or wind currents	Direction of flow
Symmetrical ripples	Wave currents in water	Trend of wave crests
Orientated 'long' fossils	Water (including wave) currents	Trend of flow or trend of wave crests
Sole structures: – flute marks	Eddying turbidity currents	Direction of flow
– groove casts	Currents dragging objects over mud	Trend of flow
Glacial striations (scratches)	Moving ice grinding rocks over bedrock	Trend of ice movement

Figure 4.2
A rose diagram of the type used in palaeocurrent analysis.
The arrow indicates the mean current direction. These measurements of current directions from
asymmetrical and symmetrical ripples were made on the sands of a modern estuary,
Sandyhaven Pill in South Wales. What was the mean direction of:
(a) the currents that produced the asymmetrical ripples;
(b) the waves that formed the symmetrical ripples?

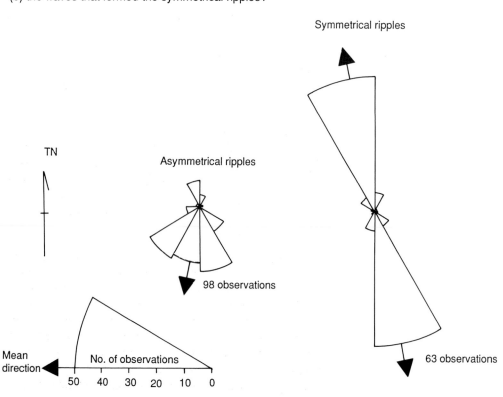

F. Geometry

A study of sedimentary environment geometry involves considering the current shape of the depositional area in three dimensions, and also investigating how the sediment is building up and out over time so that the shape of the whole volume of sediment laid down can be determined. Glacial sediments are generally deposited as lumpy 'blankets' over lowland areas whereas screes are lens-shaped. River deposits are long, fairly narrow and thin; marine deposits tend to be broad sheets over large areas of sea bed. Some typical sediment body shapes are shown in cross-section in Figure 4.3.

Figure 4.3
Cross-sections to show the typical geometries of some sedimentary bodies.
The sizes of the sediment bodies are variable. What is the possible range of sizes of each of the bodies shown?

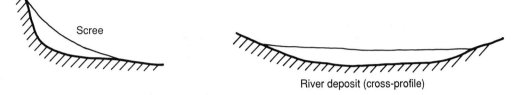

Horizontal scale variable
Vertical scale slightly exaggerated

G. The Resultant Sequence

Sediment type and structure, the fossils present and the shape of the sediment body may all, in themselves, give important clues about the ancient depositional conditions. All these factors must be considered together to develop an understanding of how the environment changes and the body of sediment grows over time. Then a picture can be determined of the whole three-dimensional body and its resultant sequence of sediments, structures and fossils.

Resultant sequences usually cannot be seen directly in modern sedimentary environments because they are too large or too thick; thus the geologist has to resort to 'model making' to put together a complete but comprehensible picture. The 'model' is not a creation that is physically built, like an aircraft model, but is rather an idea, represented in the form of diagrams and descriptions, of the type of typical sequence likely to form under certain conditions (e.g. a beach or a tidal flat). The main objective of the geologist studying modern environments is to build such a model to produce the resultant sequence that might be expected to develop over time. This can be compared with recorded sequences in ancient rocks. If the sequences are similar, the geologist has solved his problem: he has broadly interpreted and understood the ancient sedimentary environment. If there are some differences, these must be explained by further study, either of the modern environment or of the ancient sequence. If there are many differences, the geologist must 'go back to the drawing board' and research another modern environment likely to correspond with his ancient sequence.

Economic Aspects

Palaeocurrent Analysis to Find Uranium Ores

Certain uranium deposits are associated with ancient, sand-filled river channels preserved within the rock sequence. It is thought that the ores were formed from uranium-bearing fluids that flowed through the porous channel sand until a change in the chemistry of the water caused the uranium to be deposited. This happened long after the rock sequence had become buried.

When a geologist prospecting for uranium has found one of these channels, his main objective is to follow the channel until a uranium-bearing body is found. Palaeocurrent analysis allows him to discover the direction of flow of the original river water currents which are in the same direction as the channel trend where the uranium ore bodies are most likely to be located.

Oil and Gas Reservoir Shapes

When a reserve of oil or gas has been identified, the next step is to work out the shape of the reservoir. This could be done by drilling a number of boreholes at random, but this would be expensive in both time and money, and so the geologist attempts to predict the shape of the reservoir before choosing where to drill the holes.

If the reservoir has formed in a structural trap such as an anticline, the shape is fairly easy to predict, i.e. along the crest of the fold indicated by seismic work. However, if the hydrocarbon has accumulated in a stratigraphic trap, the shape and trend of the sediment body is very important and this is where the sedimentary geologist becomes a highly-valued person to the oil industry. Correct predictions can save millions!

The geologist first has to determine the environment of deposition of the sediment, from the borehole rock chippings and downhole logs. This is likely to indicate the shape of the deposit. Delta deposits, for example, are broad and thick, marine sheet sands are thin but extensive and river and coastline sequences tend to be composed of long, thin 'shoestring' sands. It is vital to determine the type and trend of shoestring sands since coastal sands lie parallel to an ancient coastline whereas river sands lie at right angles to this trend. These two types of sand body can only be distinguished from one another by detailed study of the sediments, sedimentary structures and fossils present, and by palaeocurrent analysis to give the general flow directions. When the geologist has predicted the trend of such a body, his ideas are tested by drilling further boreholes. Thus correct predictions are vital.

Practical Investigation and Fieldwork

Make your own model of a sedimentary environment

Visit a place where sediments are being deposited today. Suitable areas include screes, rivers, tidal flats, beaches and sand dunes. Study the environment using all the headings used in this chapter and, in the end, you should be able to build your own model for that sedimentary environment. Guidance on how to do this in detail can be found in other books, particularly in the sequel to this one. Take care! Modern depositional environments where processes are active can be very dangerous!

Test Your Understanding

1. List the conditions of initiation necessary for each of the following sedimentary deposits to begin forming: aeolian sand dunes; reef; beach; delta; turbidite sequence.

2. A palaeocurrent analysis has been carried out on a deposit containing symmetrical ripples. The data collected, from north, through east to south is given in the table below.

Range of Bearings	No. of Observations
000° – 029°	10
030° – 059°	07
060° – 089°	31
090° – 119°	74
120° – 149°	19
150° – 179°	03
	Total: 144

a) Plot the right-hand side of a rose diagram using the data in the table.
b) Complete the left-hand side of the diagram.
c) What is the most likely cause of the symmetrical ripples?
d) What are the most likely directions of movement of the agents that caused the ripples?
e) What is the most likely trend of the ancient coastline and/or prevailing palaeo-wind direction in the area?

3. The sedimentary succession forming the cliffs of Waterwynch Bay near Tenby in south-west Wales is of Carboniferous age. The lowest 15 metres begins at the base with a thin conglomerate which is followed by 8 metres of sandstone and then 7 metres of siltstone and mudstone. How could this sequence have been produced:

a) by a change in sediment source?
b) by a change of energy of the water currents?
c) by a complete change of the environment?

Which of these options is most likely to be correct? What further observations would help you to confirm your decision?

4. How might a geologist distinguish shoestring sands formed along a coastline from similar sands deposited by a river system?

5. FROM SEDIMENT TO SEDIMENTARY ROCK:
Processes Beneath the Surface

Diagenesis is the name given to all the physical and chemical processes that act on sediments after they become buried, excluding the metamorphism that occurs at higher temperatures and pressures. However, since diagenesis becomes low-grade metamorphism as temperatures and pressures increase, no definite line can be drawn between the two. Most diagenetic processes result in the sedimentary grains becoming bound more tightly together, resulting in the **lithification** of the sediment into rock. The effectiveness of the lithification process depends on how close individual grains become to one another: grains with few contacts with surrounding grains produce poorly lithified rocks; well-lithified rocks are the result of individual grains having many close contacts with the surrounding grains.

The diagenetic processes are closely linked with one another, but it is useful to separate them for discussion purposes.

Compaction

This physical process is caused by the mass of sediment above pressing down and squeezing the sediment beneath. How effective the overburden pressure is in squeezing the sediments, causing reductions in porosity and permeability, and resulting in the grains becoming bound more tightly together, depends greatly upon the types of sediment involved. Sediments which contain minerals that do not easily deform under pressure, such as quartz, resist compaction. However, the clay minerals that make up large proportions of most muds are very prone to compaction, and so muds become greatly compressed in the formation of mudstones as water is squeezed out.

Pressure Solution

The mass of the rock above is supported by the contacts between the grains and, at these points of extra stress where the grains are pressing together, their margins can be dissolved by the surrounding pore waters more easily. This increased solution at pressure points is called **pressure solution**. This effect may be seen particularly well in some conglomerates where pebbles have become pitted by pressure solution where other pebbles were pressing against them.

Pressure solution in limestones often produces irregular surfaces passing through the rock, called **stylolites** (see Figure 5.1). Sometimes partly dissolved fossils or ooids can be seen on one side of the stylolite, demonstrating the effectiveness of the process.

Figure 5.1
A stylolite formed by pressure solution in an ooidal limestone, as seen under the microscope.
What is the minimum amount of limestone that must have dissolved?

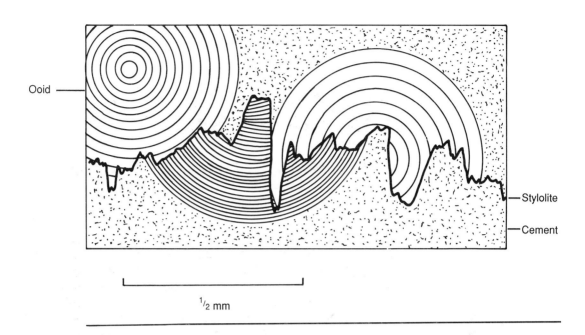

Ooid

Stylolite

Cement

$^{1}/_{2}$ mm

Quartz and calcite are particularly prone to pressure solution and the dissolved silica and carbonate produced in this way are important as the sources of cement that frequently 'glues' grains together during diagenesis.

Solution

Sedimentary particles also dissolve when the high temperatures and pressures found beneath the surface, coupled with the changes in pore-water chemistry, cause these pore waters to become powerful dissolving and transporting agents. Much dissolved matter, in the form of ions, can be transferred in this way.

The mineral aragonite, which is composed of calcium carbonate ($CaCO_3$), frequently dissolves under these conditions. Aragonite is the main component of the hard parts of many fossils; when it dissolves it leaves an imprint known as a **mould** in the sediment. Later, the moulds can be filled, usually by calcite cement, to form **casts** of the original fossils. Calcite and quartz also frequently dissolve under these conditions, particularly when they are fine grained, and so pore waters are usually rich in dissolved ions. Most of the other minerals in the sediment are also affected, to a greater or lesser degree, by the pore solutions. Some dissolve, some change, some are redeposited elsewhere; new minerals can also grow from this 'bath' of chemicals.

Recrystallisation

Recrystallisation, in the strict diagenetic sense, is the change in size or shape of a mineral during diagenesis. Calcite is the mineral most frequently involved and the most common change is the growth in size of the calcite crystals. Thus fine calcite mud frequently recrystallises to a coarse calcite mosaic and fossils which were originally calcite recrystallise, often losing much of the detail of their original structures. Fibrous calcite can also form by this process.

Replacement

This is the step-by-step change of one mineral to another. As one mineral steadily dissolves, another crystallises in its place, often preserving at least part of the original texture of the sediment. The important replacement reactions in diagenesis are described below.

A. Aragonite Replacement

Aragonite becomes replaced by its more stable **polymorph**, calcite. (Polymorphs are minerals with the same chemistry but different atomic structures and thus different mineral properties.) Aragonite is common in modern carbonate sediments and in the shells of many organisms, as ooids and as fine aragonite mud. However, these become progressively replaced by calcite, so that the older a limestone is, the more calcite it will contain.

B. Dolomitisation

Calcium carbonate sediments ($CaCO_3$) are often replaced by calcium magnesium carbonate, the mineral dolomite ($CaMg(CO_3)_2$). The process of **dolomitisation** is not well understood but there is a complete range of carbonate rocks between limestones containing less than 10 per cent dolomite to dolomites containing less than 10 per cent calcite; all the dolomite has usually been formed by recrystallisation.

C. Silification

Silification is the replacement process by which chert nodules and layers form, chert being microcrystalline quartz. These nodules or layers are generally irregular in shape and usually, as the nodule or layer grows within the rock the surrounding sedimentary layers are bent outwards. Sometimes, however, the layers can pass unaltered through the chert if it has occupied the pore spaces without displacing grains (in which case this is cementation rather than recrystallisation). The dark-coloured chert found in chalk is called flint. The source of the silica that crystallises to form chert and flint is thought to be the microscopic fragments of sponge skeletons called **spicules** that were originally deposited with the carbonate grains. These later dissolved and the silica crystallised again from the pore waters.

On occasion, fossils of calcium carbonate, and sometimes of other minerals, are replaced by silica which can preserve them beautifully. This can make them easy to remove from the rocks in which they are found.

D. Nodule Formation

Ironstone nodules which are generally oval in cross-section and round in plan view are found in some black shales, particularly Coal Measure shales. These grow as the iron carbonate mineral siderite ($FeCO_3$) steadily replaces minerals within the sediment.

Cementation

This is the growth of minerals in the gaps between the grains of sediment during diagenesis and is most important in porous and permeable rocks, i.e. those that are coarser grained. Cements crystallise from the circulating pore waters rich in the ions gained largely by dissolving minerals elsewhere.

In sandstones the two most common cements are silica and calcite. Silica cements often crystallise as **overgrowths** on the sedimentary grains of quartz present in the rocks. These overgrowths are the continuation of the atomic structure of the original quartz grains and can crystallise as well-formed crystal shapes on originally rounded grains. The original shapes of the grains can usually be seen, under the microscope, marked by a red iron or dark 'dirt' margin (see Figure 5.2). Calcite cements in sandstones may be identified by the acid (dilute HCl) test.

The crystallisation of coarse calcite cements is very important in the diagenesis of limestones and frequently, most of the original pore spaces are completely filled. This

Figure 5.2
Silica overgrowths on rounded quartz grains, as seen under the microscope.
Why do the boundaries of overgrowths often appear as straight lines?

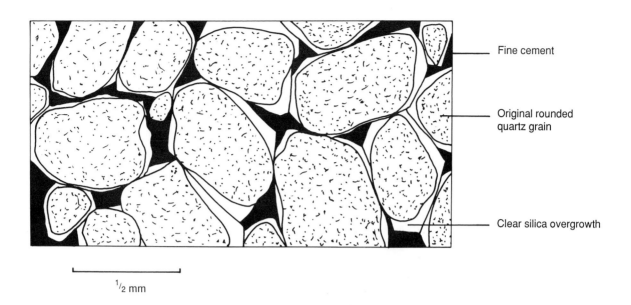

Fine cement

Original rounded quartz grain

Clear silica overgrowth

$^1/_2$ mm

reduces the porosity drastically (although secondary porosity and permeability often develop later).

Iron minerals such as red hematite (Fe_2O_3), yellow limonite ($2Fe_2O_3.3H_2O$) and brown goethite ($FeO(OH)$) may form cements on their own but are more often associated with silica and calcite cements, giving red, yellow and brown colouration to the rock. Other minerals such as barite ($BaSO_4$) and anhydrite ($CaSO_4$) can be the cementing minerals on occasion.

Note that cement should not be confused with matrix. Both cement and matrix are found between larger grains but the fine-grained matrix was deposited with the coarser grains (or may have filtered in very soon afterwards), and thus gives important clues as to the origin of the sediment. Cement, however, crystallised in the rock very much later, during diagenesis, and thus has no bearing on the original sedimentary environment. The differences are shown in Figure 5.3, but careful examination of the rock is often necessary to distinguish one from the other.

Authigenic Clay Mineral Formation

It has only recently been appreciated that new clay minerals frequently grow between sedimentary grains (particularly sandstones) either at the surface or very soon after burial. These **authigenic** (i.e. formed on the spot) clays, such as kaolinite, crystallise from the ions present in the pore fluids. The ions are present usually as the result of the breakdown of unstable minerals such as pyroxenes, amphiboles, micas and feldspars in processes similar to weathering processes (see page 8). Authigenic clay mineral deposits can greatly reduce porosity and permeability in sediments.

Rates of Diagenesis

Rates of sediment lithification vary enormously depending upon the depositional environment or the permeability of the sediment. In some tropical seas **hardgrounds**

Figure 5.3
Cement and matrix contrasted.
Why is it critical to know whether the material that 'glues together' the grains is cement or matrix?

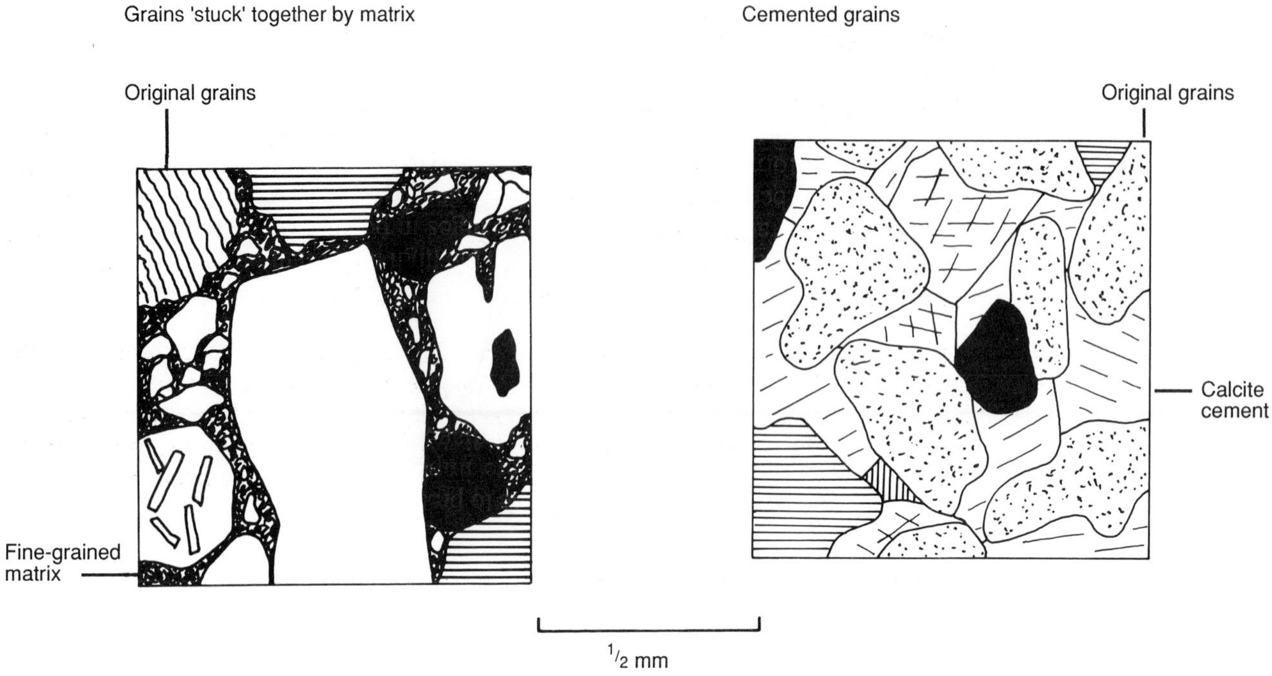

Grains 'stuck' together by matrix

Cemented grains

Original grains

Original grains

Fine-grained matrix

Calcite cement

$^1/_2$ mm

of lithified carbonate sediment have been found that contain glass bottles. Because the bottles can only be a few tens of years old, lithification must have taken place extremely rapidly in terms of geological time. Similar hardgrounds have been recognised in the geological record by the fact that they were colonised by such organisms as oysters and rock-boring animals. Oysters can only live cemented to hard rocks; rock borers live for protection in the holes they have bored into hard rocks.

However, hardgrounds are an unusual case and normally burial and long periods of geological time are necessary for the pressures, temperatures and percolating fluids to do their work of lithification. Where the fluids are unable to flow, as in impermeable rocks such as clays, little diagenesis apart from compaction takes place. Thus ancient Jurassic clays are usually still soft and muddy and the clay can be easily removed by excavators for brick making. Due to the importance of fluid flow in diagenesis, where rocks of differing permeability alternate, permeable rocks can become hard while the impermeable layers remain soft. This can be reflected in the shape of the rock face and, on a larger scale, in the surface topography.

The Sedimentary Cycle Completed

The sedimentary cycle (see page 5) is completed when buried sedimentary rocks become uplifted and exposed by erosion of the overlying rocks. The resistance of these rocks to weathering and erosion depends upon a number of factors which are directly related to the diagenetic history of the rock, such as the amount of compaction, the type and amount of cement, the amount of permeability remaining, and the stability of the remaining minerals, as shown in Chapter 2.

We have now studied all the major processes that act during the recycling of sediments in the geological cycle. The different stages of the cycle can vary greatly in extent, the lengths of time and the processes involved. This is particularly true where transportation and deposition are considered because these depend closely upon the different environments present on Earth today and in the geological past. These processes and the environments in which they work will be studied in detail in Book 2.

Economic Aspects

Swamp Deposits to Coal

Swamp environments are known as **euxinic**, i.e. they lack oxygen. This results in a very slow rate of decay of the organic material that falls into them. Since the decay products are not removed by the stagnant waters, the decay eventually stops completely. When vegetation growth is fast or long periods of time are available, thick, partially decayed swamp deposits build up, called **peat**. If the **peat** becomes buried, then diagenetic processes eventually change the peat into coal.

During the coal-forming process, known as **carbonisation** (not to be confused with the carbonation weathering process), the volatile liquids and gases contained in the organic debris are progressively driven off by heat and pressure, steadily increasing the proportion of carbon that is left behind. Since the coal formation is progressive, different types or ranks of coal are formed at different stages. This sequence, called the Coal Series, is shown in the table in Figure 5.4.

Figure 5.4
The Coal Series.
Which of these types of coal is likely to be most easy to mine in deep coal mines?

Approx. temp. of formation	*Coal type*	*% carbon*	*Description*
40°C	Peat	less than 30	Plant material still recognisable
	Lignite and similar coals	about 35–77	Hard, dull brown; plant structures still partly recognisable
70°C			
	Bituminous coal	78–90	Hard black coal with bright layers. Commonly breaks into rectangular lumps
160°C			
	Anthracite	more than 91	Hard, black, lustrous coal with conchoidal fracture

The quality of the coal improves with increasing rank and when the amount of non-organic impurities decreases. It is the impurities that form the ash produced as coal burns.

The main control on the increase of rank in coal is the temperature under the ground. The approximate temperatures at which the rank of coal changes have been calculated by careful study of coal sequences that become buried more and more deeply as they are traced beneath the ground (the temperatures can only be approximate because other processes are involved as well). The controls on the temperature are the depth of burial and the geothermal gradient of the area. Thus, where geothermal gradients are fairly normal (about 30°C per km depth), as found in some of the German coalfields, peat becomes lignite at about ½ km depth, lignite becomes bituminous coal at about 1 km depth and bituminous coal becomes anthracite at more than 5 km depth. The critical influence of temperature is shown by the fact that high rank coals can be produced by thermal metamorphism. It is because of the close link between coal rank and temperature that coal studies can give very useful guides to palaeo-temperatures in rocks during diagenesis.

Gas, and sometimes oil, can be generated during the formation of coal. These migrate up through the overlying strata and can be trapped in economically viable quantities. Coal is thus one of the important hydrocarbon source rocks.

The Formation of Oil and Gas

Oil and gas, which are both hydrocarbons, are volatiles given off from hydrocarbon source rocks during diagenesis. Coal is one of the source rocks but most of the oil and gas preserved underground has been released by the breakdown of accumulations of microscopic marine organisms called plankton. The source rocks formed in this way range from thick muds with organic matter scattered through them to black organic oozes, called **sapropels**. The key factor is that reducing conditions should not have allowed the organic matter to decay properly. On burial and diagenesis oil and gas are released as the material left behind becomes converted to **kerogen**, a rubbery, insoluble, organic substance. Different fractions of hydrocarbon are released at different temperatures, as shown in Figure 5.5.

Figure 5.5
The release of hydrocarbons (oil and gas) from source rocks with increased temperature caused by depth of burial.
At very high temperatures the methane (CH$_4$) itself breaks down. What is the likely product remaining in the source rock?

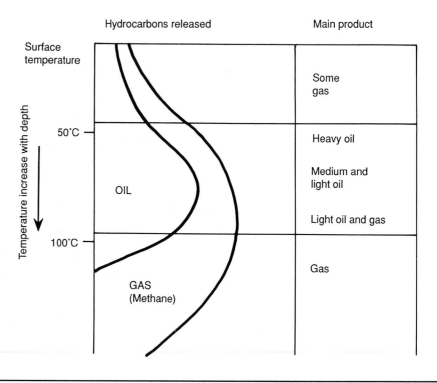

At high temperatures, the organic material becomes completely broken down to form a carbon residue. The depth at which this occurs is called the **economic basement,** because beneath this level substantial hydrocarbon accumulations are not to be expected.

The hydrocarbons are less dense than the surrounding pore waters, so as the sediments become squeezed by compaction, they migrate up through permeable overlying rocks until either they become trapped, as shown in Figure 3.21 (page 62), or they reach the surface where they are lost into the atmosphere or ocean.

Practical Investigation and Fieldwork

1. How does pressure affect sands and muds?
As you walk across a tidal flat or other area of sand and/or mud, measure and record, at intervals, the grain size of the sediment and the depth of a footprint. Plot the results on a graph. Is there any relationship between these two variables? What other processes, apart from compaction, might be operating?

2. How can sand be lithified by compaction?
Use beakers to make a series of sand castles in a tray, as follows: first use pure, damp sand pressed down hard, then use damp sand mixed with mud in varying proportions. Which sand castle was most successful: a) when just made; b) after drying? Describe and explain your results.

3. How can sand be lithified by cement?
Fill two beakers with loose sand and press down. Add distilled water to one and a supersaturated salt solution (made by stirring salt into hot water until no more will dissolve) to the other. Turn the sand castles out onto a tray and leave to dry. Describe and explain the results.

4. What is the effect of carbonisation on organic material?
Put a layer of sand in a deep metal tray, add some leaves and cover them with another good layer of sand. Place the tray in an oven at about 35°C for about 1½ hours. Remove the tray, allow it to cool and then sieve the sand. Observe the results using a hand lens or a microscope. Repeat the experiment with a less permeable material than sand and explain any contrasts in the results. (This experiment is based on one described by Scott and Collinson, 1983.)

Test Your Understanding

1. Use a copy of the table below to summarise the diagenetic effects you would expect to have been involved in the lithification of the following rocks:

an orthoquartzite (a well-sorted silica sandstone);
an ooid limestone;
a mudstone;
a fossiliferous sandy limestone (limestone with more than 50 per cent carbonate);
a deep sea limestone originally composed of tiny *Globigerina* tests made of calcite.

(The table has been filled out for a greywacke (a poorly sorted muddy sandstone) as a guide.)

Rock Type	Compaction	Pressure Solution	Recrystall-isation	Replacement	Cementation	Authigenic Mineral Formation
Greywacke	Fairly high	Some	No	No	Some	Fairly high

2. Many diagenetic changes are caused by pore waters rich in certain ions. What is/are the important ions involved in the following:

a) dolomitisation;
b) crystallising calcite cement;
c) growing ironstone nodules?

3. Which of the diagenetic processes may cause important changes in the porosity and permeability of the following potential hydrocarbon reservoir rocks:

a) porous sandstone;
b) reef limestone;
c) poorly sorted conglomerate?

4. Which of the diagenetic processes are most important in the formation of coal? Explain your answer.

5. An area has the geothermal gradient plotted in Figure 5.6.
a) Calculate the average geothermal gradient.
b) At what depths would you expect changes in rank of coal as a swamp deposit becomes progressively buried?
c) At what depths would you expect different hydrocarbons to be released as a hydrocarbon source rock becomes progressively buried?
d) At what depths would the changes (b) and (c) occur if the geothermal gradient were twice as high?

Figure 5.6
The geothermal gradient for a certain area of the Earth's crust.
What effect would this gradient have on working conditions in deep mines, i.e. those more than 1 km deep?

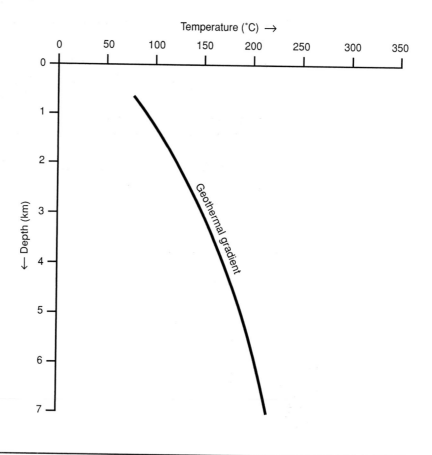

6. In the South Wales coalfield, the bituminous coals that are mined in the east are observed to pass laterally into the anthracite that is mined at the western end of the coalfield. What different explanations might there be for this change?

Further Reading

Allen, J. R. L., *Experiments in Physical Sedimentology*, Allen and Unwin, 1985.

Allen, J. R. L., *Principles of Physical Sedimentology*, Allen and Unwin, 1985.

Bateman, C., Grice, T., Richardson, G. and King, C., 'Measurement of sediment-size frequency using a burette as a settling tube', *Geology Teaching*, 8, No. 4, 1983.

Blatt, H., *Sedimentary Petrology*, Freeman, San Francisco, 1982.

Collinson, J. D. and Thompson, D. B., *Sedimentary Structures*, Allen and Unwin, 1982.

Kennett, P., 'A simulation experiment of a palaeoecological process for pupils of all ages', *Geology Teaching*, 8, No. 4, 1983.

King, C., 'Practical sedimentology for rich and poor', *Geology Teaching*, 6, No. 2, 1981.

Reading, H. G. (ed.), *Sedimentary Environments and Facies*, Blackwell, 1978.

Scott, A. and Collinson, M., 'Investigating fossil plant beds – part 2', *Geology Teaching*, 8, No. 1, 1983.

Selley, R. C., *Introduction to Sedimentology*, Academic Press, 1976.

Thompson, D., 'Experiments on porosity and permeability: part 1', *Geology Teaching*, 4, No. 1, 1979.

Tucker, M. E., *The Field Description of Sedimentary Rocks*, Open University, 1982.

Tucker, M. E., *Sedimentary Petrology: An Introduction*, Blackwell, 1981.

Watson, J., *Geology and Man*, Allen and Unwin, 1983.

Williams, P., 'On teaching physical weathering', *Geology Teaching*, 9, No. 1, 1984.

Also recommended are the following units from the Earth Science Teachers' Association, available from Geo Supplies Ltd, 16 Station Road, Chapeltown, Sheffield S30 4XH:
'Science of the Earth' units 1, 4–9, 11–12, 14, 18, 20;
'Science of the Earth 11–14' 3-unit packs: 'Sediment on the move', 'Power from the past', 'Secondhand rocks'.

Index

Each term shown in **bold type** in the index is defined on the page whose number is shown in **bold**.